NO DARKNESS AT ALL

A Biblical Defense for

Word of Faith Theology

MICHAEL MAFFUCCI

ISBN 978-1-0980-8154-6 (paperback)
ISBN 978-1-0980-8155-3 (digital)

Christian Faith Publishing, Inc.
832 Park Avenue
Meadville, PA 16335
www.christianfaithpublishing.com

Printed in the United States of America

CONTENTS

PREFACE

I would like to make it clear from the very start that my proposition in doing this dissertation is that "God is light and in Him is no darkness at all" (1 John 1:5 NKJV) My conviction is that God is never the source of death, destruction, sickness, or disease. John 10:10 (KJV) states, "The thief cometh not but for to steal, kill and destroy." It is clear from Scripture that Jesus Christ came to give life and reverse the curse of sin.

I have been teaching God's Word for more than fifty years and am very well aware of scriptures that seem to contradict the above proposition. I respect and believe that God's Word is given by His inspiration; thus, any conclusions must be solely based on the absolutes which are properly interpreted from Scripture.

Our conscience and belief system must be subject to the Word of God. If we base our belief system on our religious background, the preaching and teaching of those we respect, or even our human reasoning, we are subject to the winds of doctrine that will emasculate us from the power of Scripture.

It is very difficult to separate our thought processes from those we love and respect, and sometimes, we tend to put aside the obvious to maintain status quo. My purpose is not to offend anyone but rather to trust that God's Word will set right that which is right.

ACKNOWLEDGMENTS

I would like to give most of the credit for the completion of this book to my beloved daughter Angel who spent countless hours editing and correcting my grammar. Angel is a lady of extreme patience who put up with my frustration and all the difficulties that come with writing a book on theological issues. She is truly a gift from God. Thank you, Angel. Blessings on your head. Love, Dad.

My thanks to Pastor Murray Kartner who, in spite of his many responsibilities as administrative pastor of Agape Faith Church, put numerous hours into editing this work and added many vital suggestions to help clarify my research.

Thank you, Pastor Michael Bivins who, as a fellow instructor at Impact University, offered your time and books to help with my research. Your experience with editing for Kenneth Hagan at Rhema Bible Training center truly helped me see Brother Hagan's position on permission and secondary causation. May God restore to you one hundredfold for your time.

Thank you, my beautiful wife, Sonja (the righteous fox), for giving up our time together while I worked on this book. I sure love you!

Many thanks to my longtime friend Dr. Jason Bost for his assistance in putting this work into line for Life Christian University to complete my doctor of theology degree.

INTRODUCTION

In the movie *Billy: The Early Years*, Charles Templeton was a popular evangelist during the time that Billy Graham's ministry was beginning. Charles Templeton started out preaching the Gospel, and Bill partnered with him during the early years. The thing that struck the cords of my spirit was when Templeton began to look at all the suffering that was going on during that period and began to see God as the source of that suffering. That kind of thinking led him to doubt the inspiration of God's Word. He became a liberal professor of theology at a prestigious university and lost all faith in God.

Billy Graham, on the other hand, being dismayed at the condition of his friend, went into the woods, sat on a stump with his Bible, and met with God. He came out with the conviction that whatever the Bible says, he would believe by faith. The rest is history.

Take note that the seed of Templeton's unbelief was blaming God for something He has not done. It was the same mistake Job's wife made when she said "curse God and die." It was the same thinking behind his so-called friends when Eliphaz, Bildad, Zophar said "God is punishing you!" They even had Job convinced, until God stepped in and said, "Who is this who darkens counsel by WORDS WITHOUT KNOWLEDGE?" (Job 8:32 NKJV).

At the time of this writing, I have been a pastor for forty-one years. I have heard people blaming my God for killing their babies because someone *without knowledge* told them that God was trying to teach them something. The problem is this kind of teaching is going on in many evangelical circles today.

The purpose for this writing is to give a scriptural defense for those of us who are of the *word of faith* opinion about our God and His character and attributes. To my knowledge, there has not been such a defense which has been put into writing. For those reading this writing who do not know what I am referring to as "word of faith," I am speaking of the theology set forth beginning in Romans 10:6–11 and in the 1860s to the present with such names as E. W. Kenyon and Kenneth E. Hagin. I have also taken up this project for my students at Impact University to which I dedicate this writing and hope that they will be able to use it when their faith is attacked by "words without knowledge."

CHAPTER 1

Some Key Questions

To arrive at a proper interpretation of Scripture on this subject, I believe the following questions should be addressed:

1. If there is "no darkness AT ALL in Him" (1 John 1:5), then how could He *cause* darkness of any form to come upon people?
2. If Christ went to the cross to redeem us from sin's curse (Ephesians 2:14–18; Galatians 3:13), why would He cause sin's curse to come on people?
3. If Christ said He does *nothing* under Satan's kingdom (Matthew 12:22–28), how can we say He does?
4. If God cannot change (James 1:16–17 and Malachi 3:6), how can He give only good gifts in the New Testament and *cause* bad things in the Old Testament?
5. If God is referred to as *Jehovah Rapha*[1] in Exodus 15:26, then how can He be Jehovah with disease?
6. If heaven has no sickness or disease (Revelation 21:4–8), where would God get it to put on people?
7. If Jesus prayed "Thy will be done on earth as it is in heaven" (Matthew 6:10), why would He change that will in order to *cause* darkness to come to people?

---

[1] The God who heals.

8. If God puts sickness or destruction on you to teach or improve you, why would you want to go to a doctor and miss His will for you?

9. If the God of the Old Testament and the God of the New Testament are one and the same (Hebrews 10:7), then how can we change our hermeneutic[2] on how He works?

10. If Paul's thorn in the flesh was physical sickness, why would God not heal him when He already did at the cross (1 Peter 2:24)?

11. If physical healing was *not* part of the work of Christ on the cross (Isaiah 53:4), then why does Matthew 8:14–17 say that it was?

12. If it is impossible for God to lie (Hebrews 6:18), then how could He say that He came to give life (John 10:10) and then kill and destroy people?

---

[2] Biblical interpretation

CHAPTER 2

The Old Quaker

There is a story about an old Quaker who was sitting in his barn when two would-be robbers came in as he was sitting in his rocking chair with a loaded double-barreled shotgun aimed at the door. What he said next has much to do with *causation* and *permission*. His words were as follows: "Sirs, I would not injure thee, nor do I mean to do thee any harm, but thou art standing where I am about to shoot!" Now think about this; if the robbers were to step into the line of fire, they would be making the choice of their own volition. The Quaker gave them helpful instructions as to his intentions, but he gave them *permission* to make a choice. Had the robbers stepped into the line of fire, they would be very much dead, and the *causation* of their dilemma would have been very much their own.

Now to be sure, some slick Philadelphia lawyer would say the Quaker shot and killed them, and the Quaker could say in all honesty "I killed them." There is little doubt that the Quaker would be convicted of killing the men in a modern-day court of law, but the core question is what the *cause* of the men being shot was. Were they shot because the Quaker was aiming at them or because they stepped into the line of fire? The Quaker had established some clear *boundaries* which were not to be crossed.

Modern thinkers have great difficulty with the concept of boundaries. Dr. Henry Cloud and Dr. John Townsend make the fol-

lowing observation on the subject of boundaries in their book entitled *Boundaries*:

> The concept of boundaries comes from the very
> nature of God. God defines himself as a distinct,
> separate being, and he is responsible for himself.
> He defines and takes responsibility for his per-
> sonality by telling us what he thinks, feels, plans,
> allows, will not allow, likes, and dislikes. He also
> defines himself as separate from his creation and
> from us. He differentiates himself from others. He
> tells us who he is and who he is not. For example,
> he says that he is love and that he is not darkness
> (1 John 4:16; 1:5). In addition, he has set bound-
> aries within the Trinity. The Father, the Son, and
> the Spirit are one, but at the same time they are
> distinct persons with their own boundaries. Each
> one has his own personhood and responsibilities,
> as well as a connection and love for one another
> (John 17:24). God also limits what he will allow
> in his yard. He confronts sin and allows conse-
> quences for behavior. (*Boundaries*, 35)

Why is it that most people are reticent to take personal responsibility for the things they do? Perhaps it is easier to shift the blame of
our circumstance onto someone else. Now let's get back to the story
of the old Quaker sitting in his barn with a loaded shotgun aimed at
the barn door and ready to shoot. This story illustrates very nicely the
sense of what is being said. For example, the Ten Commandments,
which are given in Exodus, chapter 20, are not the "Ten Suggestions."
It is God telling man the direction in which He is shooting. When
men step into the line of fire, God rightly says I kill, but He is not
the cause of their action of transgression. He is simply shooting in
the direction of who He is and what His holiness requires. God is not
the *cause*; He simply is what He is. One must also remember that He
says "I kill and I make alive" (Deuteronomy 32:39). He makes alive

in the same sense as He does when He says I kill. People receive His life and are "born of God" when they make the volitional choice to receive Christ as their Lord and Savior. God indeed makes alive, but it is because someone has stepped into who Christ is.

At this point, someone usually says to me, "So you think they died because they sinned against God!" A statement like that is over-looking the contributing factors of the variables that can bring about the circumstances in any given situation. For example, God's word states in Hosea 4:6, "My people are destroyed for lack of knowledge. Because you have rejected knowledge, I also will reject you from being priest for Me; Because you have." The following ideas reflect this lack of knowledge:

1. One can step into the line of fire of God's commandment as we have just suggested.
2. One can have a wrong scriptural idea that it is God's will that you die from some dreaded disease.
3. One can get into fear like Job did when he got out of faith, and his hedge came down. "The thing that I greatly feared has come upon me" (Job 3:25). Of course, we know who was after Job. Satan hated him because of his godly life.
4. One may not know the covenant, or one may reject prom-ises that promise you *healing* (Psalm 103:3), *long* life (Psalm 91:16), *health* (3 John 2).
5. One may be speaking death words over yourself and, thereby, giving Satan permission to destroy you. "Life and death are in the power of your tongue" (Proverbs 18:21). Satan can do *nothing* without your authoritative permis-sion, even as a Christian. "Satan...seeking whom he MAY devour" (1 Peter 5:8). The Greek word used here for *devour* is *katapeiin* which is the second aor.act infinitive which means he wants to destroy, devour, engulf, annihilate your lunch, and pop the bag when he is finished with it.
6. The *Amplified Bible* says, one may be nullifying and mak-ing void and of no effect (the authority of) the Word of God through your tradition.

The list can go on and on, so it is not our job to judge any person or any event that may happen. Our responsibility is to know the Word of God and believe what it has to say.

Now let's talk about the real cause of darkness, death, and destruction. The Bible says that we are to be aware of the wiles of the devil.

"Put on the whole armor of God that you may be able to stand against the wiles of the devil" (Ephesians 6:11). The word *wiles* comes from the Greek word *methodeias* which is the word we get our English word *methods* from. The devil would love to have every believer to step into the line of fire of our God's holiness. His usual methods of attack are the lust of the flesh, the lust of the eyes, and the pride of life according to 1 John 2:16. When a believer falls into one of these traps and begins to reap what he has sown, the deceiver then enjoys getting the believer to think that God is the source of his grief. Job is a good example of this process. When Job got into fear, his hedge of protection came down (Job 1:12). When Satan attacked Job, what was the outcome? His wife said "curse" *God* (Job 2:9). Eliphaz said it was the blast of *God* (Job 4:9). Bildad the Shuhite said *God* has cast you away (Job 8:20). Zophar the Naamathite said *God* exacts from you (Job 11:6). Job answered them correctly when he said in a sarcastic comment "no doubt you are the people, and wisdom will die with you" (Job 12:2).

Job's witty comment makes us laugh, but are we not doing the same thing as his three "friends" when we say God is putting sickness or disease on someone to *teach* them something? How can anyone believe God in faith for healing if he thinks God is putting that sickness on him? I do not want to be mean-spirited in any way, but if you believe that it is God's will to have you sick or to teach you something, then do not go to a physician, or you will not learn what you need to learn! The Bible is very clear that "instruction in righteousness and correction" (2 Timothy 3:16) is to come from the word of God. How many of God's people have died because of rejecting this concept? (See Hosea 4:6.)

In *Christ the Healer*, F. F. Bosworth quotes from a prominent speaker of his day who believed that God put sickness on people to teach them more about His grace.

> The fact is Paul was sick; He was the SICKEST of men. He had one of the most painful oriental diseases. He had Ophthalmia, a disease of the eyes. The proof that he had it is overwhelming. He tells us that he had a "thorn in the flesh." When Paul stood before Christians his eyes filled with unspeakable pus, unspeakable-looking matter running down over his face. Why would they gouge out their eyes for him except that his eyes, as he stood before them, were a pitiable and appealing sight to them, as the eyes of anyone with Ophthalmia are? The particular pain of this disease is like a "stake" in the eyes. It is beyond dispute that Paul was a sick man. He says so himself. Paul did not get this disease by infection. How did he get it? Jesus Christ GAVE IT TO HIM. (*Christ the Healer*, 203–204).

I would like to bring out two things of note at this point. Firstly, the Bible says most clearly that this was not of God but rather "a messenger OF SATAN." Secondly, "thorn in the flesh" is a Hebrew idiom that is never used for physical sickness. It only refers to persecution from a person or a nation. (See Numbers 33:55 and Joshua 23:13.)

We must be impeccably honest with the way we handle the Word of God. It must be handled in an accurate and consistent manner. Otherwise, we become guilty of eisegesis[3] rather than exegesis[4] of God's word. We as the church cannot afford to use a proof text, as do many of the cults, to prove a preconceived bias on a subject. We

---

[3]   Read into the Word.
[4]   Take out of the Word.

must go to the Word with an open heart and let the scriptures speak for themselves.

When I first came to North Carolina in the late eighties, I was one of the few pastors in this area who preached the uncompromised Word. I was teaching on the subject of healing on a local radio station Word got around that I believed it is always God's will to heal, and I developed quite a reputation among the local pastors as a real *faith fanatic*. One day, a friend of mine informed me of a young lady from our area who had cancer and was about to die from its effects. My heart went out to her and her family, so I made a special trip to Baptist Hospital in Winston-Salem to pray for her recovery. Upon arriving at the intensive care room where she was being treated, I was given a very cold greeting from the young lady's family and the religious friends that were gathered for her homegoing. I suppose someone had informed them of my coming. When I asked if I could pray for her healing, I was refused and asked to leave. They had been taught that God had put this dreaded disease on that young lady, and it was time for her to go home because God needed her in heaven. A short time later, she did die but not because God put that disease on her. It was God's will to heal her, but wrong teaching closed the door for her deliverance. If you do not believe it is God's will to heal you, how can you have faith that He will heal you? If you believe God has put cancer on you, how can you ask in faith for your healing?

CHAPTER 3

"He Who Has Seen Me Has Seen the Father" (John 14:9)

Marcion, who was a second-century heretic, had a great deal of difficulty dealing with the above statement of Jesus. He could not come to grips with the idea that the God of the New Testament was the same God in the Old Testament. Because of his radical concept, he took it upon himself to purge the New Testament of any scripture which equated the God of the Old Testament with the God of the New Testament. His views were so radical that it was one of the major causes for the early church to developing a rule of canon that would recognize which books of the Bible were in fact inspired of God.

The New International Dictionary of the Christian Church states:

> Marcion stressed the radical nature of Christianity vis-à-vis Judiasm.* In his theology there existed a total discontinuity between the OT and the NT, between Israel and the church, and even between the God of the OT and the father of Jesus. Jesus came to reveal the true God, who was totally unknown up to the incarnation. The god of the OT, the demiurge,[5]* an inferior being who created the material world and ruled over it, was not exactly an evil being, but he was not good in the

---

[5] A subordinate deity

same sense as the God and Father Jesus, a God of
love and grace. (629)

If one is to follow the teachings of the Bible, the character of
Jesus cannot be different than the character of His Father. Although
their roles are different, God the Father would not do anything that
God the Son would not do and vice versa. They are one in purpose
and method of operation. "Christ came that we might have life and
that more abundantly" (John 10:10). If Christ is a life giver, then His
Father must, by virtue of their sameness, be a life giver. To be a life
giver and a death giver are incompatible. To be a healer and to put
diseases on people is also incompatible.

First Peter 2:24 tells us "who himself bore our sins in his own
body on the tree, that we having died to sins, might live for righteousness by whose stripes you were healed." We know that this scripture deals with physical healing because Jesus fulfilled it in Matthew
8:14–17.

Here are some other important scriptures which tell us that the
Father and the Son are exactly one in purpose and method.

No one has seen God at any time. The only
begotten Son, WHO IS IN THE BOSOM OF THE
FATHER has declared Him." (John 1:18; emphasis
added)

Philip said unto him, "Lord show us the way
and it is sufficient for us." Jesus said unto him,
"Have I been with you so long, and yet you have
not known me, Phillip? He who has seen me has
seen the Father; so how can you say 'show us
the Father'? Do you not believe that I am in the
Father, and the Father in me? The words that I
speak to you I do not speak on my own authority; but the Father who dwells in Me DOES THE
WORKS. Believe me that I am in the Father and
the Father in me, or else believe me for the sake

of THE WORKS THEMSELVES." (John 14:8–11
NKJV; emphasis added).

He is the image of the invisible God, the first-
born over all creation. (Colossians 1:15)

For it pleased the Father that in Him all the fullness should dwell. (Colossians 1:19)

For in Him dwells ALL THE FULLNESS OF THE
GODHEAD BODILY. (Colossians 2:9)

Herein lies the dilemma I submit that one must deal with in
order to have a proper hermeneutic[6] of the Old and New Testament.
If Jesus, the Son, came to give life, how can God the Father say "I kill
and I make alive" (Deuteronomy 32:39)?

A proper hermeneutic teaches us that the scriptures cannot contradict themselves. We must also interpret unclear scriptures by the
clear passages over the unclear, knowing that there must be a proper
interpretation that will not contradict.

Since Jesus, the Son, does not operate in the kingdom of darkness according to Matthew 12:25–28 which clearly deals with sickness, blindness, and the mute, how can God the Father say He put
these diseases on the enemies of Israel? Exodus 15:26 says, "I will put
none of the diseases on you that I HAVE BROUGHT ON the Egyptians.
For I am the Lord who heals you."

In his book on *Seven Things You Should Know about Divine
Healing*, Kenneth E. Hagin makes the following observation concerning Exodus 15:26: "The Hebrew literally reads 'I will PERMIT none
of these diseases upon thee, which I permitted upon the Egyptians'"
(17). This interpretation would change the verb usage from *causative*
to *permissive*. Causation puts the action and the source of disease as
coming from God which appears to contradict the clearer scriptures
in Matthew 12:25–28. Jesus indicates clearly that God does not con-

---

6   Biblical interpretation

tradict or oppose himself. What God permits because of free will shows the results of people making wrong choices.

Since my area of expertise is in teaching New Testament Greek and not in Hebrew, I have gone to the scholarship of Dr. Spiros Zodhiates's book *The Complete Word Study Old Testament* to determine the grammatical usage of this and other similar Old Testament texts.

Where Exodus 15:26 says "I will put," it is the Hebrew verb *sum* or *sim* which is grammatically the *qal* stem.[7] In Dr. Zodhiates's book, the following statement is made on the qal stem:

> The QAL stem can be divided into two main classes: verbs that represent action [fientive] and verbs that describe a state of being [stative]. Scholars disagree as to whether a passive counterpart to the QAL stem exists in the Hebrew language. (*The Complete Word Study Old Testament*, 2282)

The point is that this verse can go either way; therefore, its meaning must be determined by context and still be grammatically correct.

Thus, in light of these sound principles of hermeneutics, the interpretation must be that one does not contradict the clear teachings of other scripture. So in this scripture, the correct interpretation would seem to make it permissive rather than causative.

In order to be more accurate, look with me at a similar verse in Deuteronomy 32:29 where God says "I Kill." The Hebrew word is *muth*.

> The Scriptures present death as unnatural, as something which God did not want to happen, but which came about as a RESULT of sin [Genesis 3:3]. God takes no pleasure in it [Ezekiel 18:32].

---

[7] In grammar, a stem is the basic word form.

> A holy God must separate himself from anything which is not IN HARMONY WITH HIS CHARACTER. (Zodhiates, 2330)

The Hebrew stem being used here is the *hiphil* imperfect tense.

> Though in the English language the idea of CAUSATION seems always to be a matter of compulsion, the CAUSATIVE sense of the HIPHEL can represent less direct ideas, such as the granting of PERMISSION to do a certain thing. (p. 2274)

If you take this grammatical statement which comes from Hebrew scholarship and compare it with the clear teachings of the New Testament, would it not make more sense to translate it as *permissive* rather than *causative*? Another difficult passage that deals with permission and causation is how God dealt with the pharaoh of Egypt. Without a careful reading of the text, it would appear at first that God is causing the heart of the pharaoh to be hardened so as to allow the ten plagues to come upon him. That being the case, it would make God the cause of pharaoh's problems.

Much modern and liberal theology that has a perverted view of inspiration tries to rewrite the chronology of this account to make it less *supernaturalistic*. The teaching known as the documentary theory, or JEDP theory, was established by Julius Wellhausen.

Geisler and Nix's *A General Introduction to the Bible* states:

> They actually attempted to mediate between traditionalism and skepticism, dating the Old Testament books in a less super naturalistic manner by applying the "documentary theory." These documents are identified as the Jahovistic [J], dated in the ninth century BC, Elohistic [E], dated about a century later, Deuteronomic [D], from the time of Josiah (640–609 BC), and the

Priestly [P], from perhaps the fifth century BC. (437)

It is so much easier to accept the inspired text as it is. A careful reading of the text from Exodus 7–10 will demonstrate the chronology of how it actually took place.

1. Exodus 7:3 gives us a prophetic overview of the entire scene. God says "I will harden," and He uses the *piel*[8] imperfect tense, but He does not say *when* He would harden his heart.
2. "It was not until the seventh plague that Yahweh made Pharaoh's heart hard."
3. In the five previous plagues, Pharaoh hardened his own heart.
4. It was his own volition that preceded and determined the course of God's action.

Is that not the same thing that will happen to those who miss the rapture who "did not receive the love of the truth, that they might be saved. For this reason God will send them strong delusion, that they should believe *the lie* (2 Thessalonians 2:10–11)?

God's great mercy is reaching out to the lost in our dispensation, but at the rapture, those who did not receive the love of the truth (or if you will, those who rejected the clear gospel message) cannot be part of the tribulation saints because of their own volitional choice before the rapture. God sends them delusion because of their previous choices. He was not the cause, but he permitted them to choose.

Why does God seem so loving in the New Testament and so angry in the Old Testament? Since Jesus and the Father are exactly one in purpose and method, why the difference in appearance? The truth is that both Testaments are in complete agreement with each other when you look at the context of each issue. Kaiser brings out three important points that shed more light on the subject in his book *Hard Sayings of the Bible*.

---

[8] See chapter 7 for more information on the piel stem

First, there is love in the Old Testament. God does not present Himself first and foremost as a God of judgment but as a God of love. For example, look at Exodus 34:6–7:

> And he passed in front of Moses, proclaiming, "The Lord, the Lord, the compassionate and gracious God, slow to anger, abounding in love and faithfulness, maintaining love to thousands, and forgetting wickedness, rebellion and sin. Yet he does not leave the guilty unpunished; he punishes the children and their children for the sin of the fathers to the third and fourth generation." (Exodus 34:6–7)

Second, there is judgment in the New Testament. A word count on judge or judgment in the New Testament comes up with 108 verses. Even more significant is the fact that Jesus is the one who warns most about judgment. Third, there is a difference between the Testaments in their portrayal of judgment. In the Old Testament, judgment normally happens within history. When Israel sins, they are not told that they will go to hell when they are raised from the dead but that they will be punished by the Midianites or Assyrians. So does the Old Testament reveal a God of judgment and the New Testament a God of love? Emphatically, no. Both of the Testaments reveal a God of love who is also a God of justice. God offers men and women His love and forgiveness, urging us to repent and escape the terrible and eternal judgments of the end of history.

There are other numerous passages in the Old Testament which appear to make God the ogre and not the redeemer, and I am reticent to try to deal with each one of them in particular in this section. But I have found that all of these are in harmony with the life and methods of the Christ of the New Testament. That is why Jesus said "Have I been with you so long, and yet you have not known Me, Philip? He who has seen Me has seen the Father; so how can you say, 'Show us the Father'?" (John 14:9 NKJV).

In conclusion, I submit that one must choose between one of the four varied viewpoints on this issue:

1. One might say God acted differently in the Old Testament because it was before the new covenant. Thus, God could be one thing under the old covenant and something else under the new covenant.
2. One could adopt the heretical Marcion theology of the second century and say there are two different gods.
3. One could go with the dualistic Manichaeistic[9] theology of the fourth century and try to ransack the Old Testament of all the examples of offensive morality.
4. One could use a proper hermeneutic and realize that what God *permits* in the Old Testament is under secondary causation by Him and is based on the volitional choices of individuals and nations.

It is important to realize at this point that God does not give us His good gifts because of our own merit. While wrong choices do open us up to destruction from the enemy, good choices do not qualify us for God's grace. Grace is always a result of God's agape love which cannot be earned.

---

[9] Manichean rewrote the Old Testament to fit his theology.

CHAPTER 4

Schoolmaster and Shadow Theology

One of the main principles of proper hermeneutical interpretation is to interpret the less clear passages of scripture by the passages which are clearer. One of the main ploys used in the cults is to take an obscure scripture or a scripture which is unclear and read it out of context and turn it into a doctrine. A person can twist the scriptures into any doctrine that they want by using obscure scriptures.

Peter alludes to this practice when he says, "as also in all his epistles, speaking in them of things, in which are some things hard to understand, which untaught and unstable people TWIST to their own destruction, as they do also the rest of the Scriptures" (2 Peter 3:16 NKJV).

I have a very beautiful wife. When Sonja walks in the sunshine, she casts a lovely shadow. To look at her shadow makes me want to turn and look at her real form. As lovely as her shadow is, there is no way I can see her beautiful green eyes by looking at her silhouette. Sonja's shadow cannot come close to demonstrating her lovely features. The best I can do with that scenario is to imagine her features by what I see in her shadow. To try to make a defined mental or physical picture of what she is really like from looking at her obscure shadow would be absurd. All I have to do to see what she is really like is to look at her face.

The Bible tells us that the Old Testament law is a shadow of things to come, but the real substance is of Christ. Paul says, "So let no one judge you in food or drink or regarding a festival or a new moon or Sabbaths which are a SHADOW of things to come, but the SUBSTANCE is Christ" (Colossians 2:16–17 NKJV).

I submit that it is not only dangerous but also hermeneutically improper to try to give God an attribute that does not line up with New Testament teaching. God is never the cause of death, nor the source of darkness in the New Testament. How can He be anything other than life and light in the Old Testament when both Testaments are inspired by God and inerrant? Proper interpretation demands congruency between the Testaments. His Old Testament shadow cannot fully determine His New Testament image. His New Testament image must complete what His Old Testament character had begun.

God is not reticent, as many of today's psychologically misinformed parents, to allow people to feel the consequences of their own misdeeds. While God is *not* causative of the results people experience by going their own way, God does let them serve the gods that they choose.

> Therefore God GAVE THEM UP to uncleanness, in the lust of their hearts, to dishonor their bodies among themselves. (Romans 1:24 NKJV)

> For this reason God GAVE THEM UP to vile passions. For even their women exchanged the natural use for what is against nature. (Romans 1:26 NKJV)

> And even as they did not like to retain God in their knowledge. God GAVE THEM OVER to a debased mind, to do those things which are not fitting. (Romans 1:28 NKJV)

Notice that all of these statements show God as permissive. He is giving them the result of their own volitional choice. He is not causing their destruction. He is permitting the law of sin and death to go into operation (see Romans 9). He is not the law of sin and death; He is the law of the spirit of life. Once again, we see how death is the reciprocal of life. In the preceding scriptures, their death *choices* brought them into the line of fire. Did God cause their problem? No, He did not!

> Did God turn them over to their continuous choices? Yes, He did. Was He the one who brought their destruction? No, He was not. God's boundaries are designed for our good. To transgress His boundaries is to receive what is on the other side of His property line, death. Boundaries are personal property lines that define who you are and who you are not, and influence all areas of your life. Physical boundaries help you determine who may touch you and under what circumstances. Mental boundaries give you the freedom to have your own thoughts and opinions. Emotional boundaries help you deal with your own emotions and disengage from the harmful, manipulative emotions of others. Spiritual boundaries help you distinguish God's will from your own and give you renewed awe for your creator. (Cloud and Townsend)

God is not the cause of man's miserable condition. Jesus came that "we might have life" (John 10:10 NKJV).

> And this is the condemnation that the light has come into the world, and men loved darkness rather than light, because their deeds were evil. (John 3:19–20 NKJV)

The Old Testament law was a *shadow* of the good things to come but not the very image of those things.

> For the law, having a shadow of the good things to come, and not the very image of the things, can never with these same sacrifices which they offer continually year by year, make those who approach perfect. (Hebrews 10:1)

We know from looking at the Old Testament sacrifices that they were in themselves not the answer to man's sin problem but only an act of faith that God would provide Himself a lamb. The Old Testament lamb which was a portrayal of that Lamb which was to come was not a perfect picture of Him but only a shadow. The Apostle John called Him the "Lamb of God" (John 1:29), but he certainly did not mean to imply that he looked like a sheep! Jesus was in fact the fulfillment of that shadow, and He was most assuredly the Lamb of God. The point is this. If we rashly make a theology out of what the Old Testament appears to say that God is doing, are we not making a theology out of shadow instead of looking at the clear choice of the cross?

CHAPTER 5

God's Kingdom Cannot Be Divided (Matthew 12:25)

I have done a careful exegesis of the above scriptures, and to the best of my ability and knowledge of the original Greek language, I have tried to use a proper hermeneutic in interpreting it's meaning. These scriptures contain one of the most clear-cut distinctions in the Word of God of the two kingdoms: The kingdom of darkness and its substance is lucidly described. The kingdom of God and its content are vividly portrayed.

History shows us that in World War II, a great line of distinction was drawn between what was known as the Axis powers of Germany, Italy, and Japan and the Allied powers. Both sides of this great conflict were absolutely opposed to each other. It was a time of tremendous worldwide upheaval for nations and families. Success finally came to the Allied forces under Dwight D. Eisenhower, whose abilities as a general brought the Axis powers to their knees and ended the conflict.

Can you imagine the difference it would have made if any of the Allied nations would have taken sides with the Axis powers? You might now have German or Japanese as your native language. You see, a kingdom divided cannot stand. This reasoning is the point our Lord is making in this portion of scripture.

Now let's look at the two kingdoms described in the text. Let's call them *Kingdom Darkness* and *Kingdom Light* so we can delineate proper sides. In Matthew 12:22, we see the ravages and content of Kingdom Darkness:

1. Demon possessed
2. Blind
3. Mute

Compare the above to Kingdom Light.

1. He healed him.
2. The blind saw.
3. The mute spoke.

Jesus is literally fulfilling the prophetic words about His kingdom in Isaiah 42:7–8 and Isaiah 35:5–6. Consider how these scriptures answer the interrogative of John the Baptist in Matthew 11:3–5.

> To open the eyes of the blind, to bring out prisoners from the prison, those who sit in darkness from the prison house. (Isaiah 42:6)

> Then the eyes of the blind shall be opened, and the ears of the deaf shall be unstopped. Then the lame shall leap like a deer, and the tongue of the dumb shall sing. (Isaiah 35:5–6)

> And he said to Him, "Are You the Coming One, or do we look for another?" Jesus answered and said to them, "Go tell John the things which you hear and see; the blind see and the lame walk; the leapers are cleansed and the deaf hear; the dead are raised up and the poor have the gospel preached to them." (Matthew 11:3–5 NKJV)

The question being asked by John contains more than meets the eye in the New King James text. When John said "do we look for ANOTHER?" he was asking a very important question in the Greek.

The word *another* can be written as *allos* (another of the same kind), or it can be written as *heteros* (another of a different kind). John was literally asking, are we looking for a king of a *different* kind?

The Pharisees accused Jesus of doing these things by the power of another kingdom. They accused Him of working with Satan's kingdom. Notice the answer that Jesus gave.

> Every kingdom divided against itself is brought to desolation, and every city or house divided against itself will not stand. If Satan casts out Satan, he is divided against himself. How then will his kingdom stand?… But if I cast out demons by the Spirit of God, surely the KINGDOM OF GOD has come to you. (Matthew 12:25–28 NKJV)

The phrase "divided against itself" is actually one word in the Greek. The word is *meristheisa* which happens to be a nominative singular feminine participle first aorist passive of the verb *merizo*. With this construction, the action of the verb comes back on the subject. Jesus tells John, "I am fulfilling scripture by directly opposing Satan's kingdom." Do you see the point? God *does not* use Satan's kingdom to accomplish His work!

Satan's kingdom never comes to the light because it cannot stand the light. God's kingdom has no darkness at all in it because God hates darkness. "This is the message which we heard from Him and declare to you, that God is light and in Him is NO DARKNESS AT ALL" (John 1:5 NKJV). It is impossible to get around the fact that the kingdom of light and the kingdom of darkness are opposing forces that do not mix. John's gospel puts it under further scrutiny. "In Him was life, and the life was the light of men. And the light shines in the darkness, and the darkness did not comprehend it" (John 1:4–5 NKJV). The word *comprehend* is the Greek word *katelambano*, and it ordinarily means "to grasp, seize, win, or attain," but according to Arndt and Gingrich, it takes a different translation in this verse. "Most Greek commentators since Origen take katelambano here as overcome, suppress" (414).

Light overcomes darkness every time, and darkness cannot overcome light. The fact is, the greater the darkness, the greater the effect of the light. The Genesis account of the creation is another good example of this law:

> The earth was without form and void; and darkness was on the face of the deep. And the Spirit of God was hovering over the face of the waters. Then God said, "Let there be light"; and there was light. And God saw the light that it was good; and God DIVIDED THE LIGHT from the darkness." (Genesis 1:2–4 NKJV)

The very first act of God over a formless earth was to create light. This was done even before He made the sun, moon, and stars on the fourth day. God made the light on day one and said it was good. It is also significant that God divided the light from the darkness. In nature, light and darkness are opposites, and the same is true in the spiritual realm.

Would it not be mixing two kingdoms for God to reach over into Satan's kingdom to put some of his sickness and disease on a person to teach them something? Death, sickness, disease, destruction, guilt, condemnation, and anything else negative is a result of the fall. Satan's kingdom is a warped perversion and counterfeit of God's kingdom. It is opposed to anything that is of God. On the opposite end is God's kingdom which is right, the truth, and the way.

The throne of God and the heavenly realm contains no sickness, death, or disease. The effects of the curse do not exist in heaven.

> And God will wipe away every tear from their eyes; there will be no more death, nor sorrow, nor crying. There will be no more pain, for the

former things have passed away. (Revelation 21:4 NKJV)

Jesus asked us to pray that His will be done on earth as it is in heaven (Matthew 6:10 NKJV).

CHAPTER 6

What If Someone Doesn't Get Healed?

What if someone does not get healed? What if they die? What about so and so who is such a great Christian, and they are still in a wheelchair? The theology of doubt and unbelief goes on and on with declarations of unbelief. It is amusing how our preconceived ideas are displayed by what we are convinced of. On June 10, 1992, the Lord showed me the following insight as I was meditating on Philippians 4:13.

"Convinced" (Philippians 4:13)

David was too young to understand
the theology that said
"It cannot be done."

The theology of impossibility
has never changed.
but the giant is still dead!

David's success came by the
Action of his belief.

Things that never get done for God
Are a result of our unbelief and
not because of the youth of our faith.

Hence, all accomplishments come because
We are convinced that we can.
"I can do all things through Christ."

Right or wrong "Convinced" is the
Opposite of confusion:
It is the substance of faith.
It is the catalyst for action.
It is the courage of all endeavors.
If the substance is Truth
The result will be success!

If the substance is error
The result will be failure.

The spirit of Truth and Error
Are the variables. 1 John 4:6

I do not want to sound hateful or prideful to those of you who do not agree with this kind of thinking. But I must ask the question: Is it not possible that much of the sterile, uninfectious theology is a result of the desire to explain away the deadness of our faith? Are our giants not slain because God does not want us to slay them or because our theology has brought us to the place of *comfortable unbelief?* Worse yet, do we believe that God does not want the giants slain? What if we think God is the giant? Why go to the brook to get our five smooth stones if it is not God's will to kill the giants. Five giants fell by the hand of David in 2 Samuel 21:22 because he was *convinced* that they would!

"Expect"

Many who are born with bodies complete
have paralyzed spirits
and go down in defeat.

That which is in them is causing
their hurt
because with destruction
and sin they will flirt.

Their bodies with sickness and disease
are taunted
Because the love and the knowledge of God
they have flaunted.

Although you were born with attack
from the fire
within you is God's spirit
that's greater and higher.

Though the battle is heavy
and the time seems long
God's Word within you says:
"Weak, I am strong."

Within you is strength
that no mortal can muster
shake off your shoes
and the enemy duster.

All things are possible
to those who believe
look at your Savior
and your strength He'll retrieve.

Cerebral Palsy was given a name
at the feet of Jesus
it must bow in shame.

Desiring a miracle
on His Word I reflect.

And this is the answer
from what I detect.

To receive from the Father
one word I project.
Within it is your answer
the word is "Expect." Mark 9:23

At the time of this writing, my wife and I have nine children and thirty-four grand- and great-grandchildren. Our last three children are adopted and have caused Sonja and myself to stay perpetually young! Two of our adopted children were born with cerebral palsy (CP) and are presently in power wheelchairs. They are unable to function with full motor control. CP is caused by traumatic damage to the cerebral part of the brain. It is often caused by birth trauma or physical accident. The point is, CP is a form of brain damage that is physically irreversible. Angel, who is now thirty-three years old, has an associate's degree in psychology from Liberty University. She is a highly intelligent young lady. At the present time, she is working on her bachelor of arts degree at Impact University. I am addressing this subject to demonstrate the difference between healing, which is an established fact, and that which has been provided for by Christ's atonement.

> But He was wounded for our transgressions; He was bruised for iniquities. The chastisement of our peace was upon Him and by His stripes we WERE HEALED. (Isaiah 5:35)

> When evening had come, they brought to Him many who were demon possessed. And He cast out the spirits with a word, and healed all who were sick, that it might be fulfilled which was spoken by Isaiah the prophet saying, "He Himself took our infirmities and BORE our sicknesses."

Now the Bible makes a difference between healing, as demonstrated by the above verses, and the gift of miracles in 1 Corinthians 12:10. "The working of miracles," *energea*, is energy-releasing power. This happens "as He wills" (1 Corinthians 12:11.) Both Angel and Perla know they are healed, but the manifestation of a recreative miracle works as the Holy Spirit's timing wills. It comes as a result of *expectancy*. I gave Angel the above poem on her twelfth birthday on March 28, 1992. It was given to me from Mark 9:23. "Jesus said to him, 'If you can believe, all things are possible to him who believes.'"

Of course, it is not up to us to try to figure out God's timing; we are not to judge anyone but ourselves when it comes to our faith. The manifestation is for an appointed time. However, to turn things around and say that God put that awful form of brain damage on Angel or Perla is entirely unwarranted by scriptural teaching. While we wait for any manifestation of God's power, we must speak God's word in faith and *expect* Him to do what He says.

CHAPTER 7

A Brief Tutorial on Biblical Languages

One of the professors at Impact University who specializes in thesis writing is Murray Kartanson. Murray is a man of tremendous wisdom and stability. "The lips of the righteous feed many" (Proverbs 10:21). Murray is that kind of a man. He spent many hours reading and making suggestions that have strengthened and added invaluable information to this dissertation. One of Murray's recommendations was to insert a brief teaching for the benefit of those who are unfamiliar with biblical languages and how they differ from the English language. As I have stated earlier, my field of biblical language is New Testament Greek. I have been teaching Greek at Impact University since 2008, and consequently, when I start speaking about language, case usage, and syntax, I forget that most people are unfamiliar with how grammar works in different languages.

To begin, let us consider verbs. In English, verbs have the following qualities:

> *Tense.* The main purpose of tense as we understand it is to show the time in which an action is taking place, and so we have past, present, and future tense.
>
> *Voice.* Voice indicates the relation of the subject to the action. When we use the active voice, the subject is acting. Thus, the action of the verb is actually com-

ing from the subject. When we use the passive voice, the subject is being acted upon.

In English grammar, we must construct our sentences in such a way that the reader will see the action as being active or passive by the actual construct of the sentence. For example, to show the active construct of a situation, we would say "a fireman is spraying water on the fire." To show the passive construct we would say, "a fireman is being sprayed by water after it hit the fire." In New Testament Greek and in Hebrew, the action of voice is shown within the construction of the verb being used. The verb itself changes form to show if it is active or passive. A basic example of this is the Greek sentence for the active voice where the subject of the sentence loses something in the future. In English, we would say "I shall loose the chains." In the Greek structure, rather than use three words "I shall loose," one can just use one word, *luso*. The *lu* is the stem of the word loose, the *s* makes it future, and the *o* makes it first person singular. The word *luso* is in the active voice which makes the action of the verb come from the subject, *I*. So the one-word *luso* says, "I shall loose." That one word is future, active, first person, singular. There is also one word that says "I shall be loosed" which is the word *luthesomai*. The *lu* is the stem of the word *loose* that makes it future; *omai* makes it first person singular. The word *luthesomai* is in the passive voice which causes the action of the verb go to the subject, *I*. That one word is future, passive, first person, singular.

The preceding may sound rather complicated to those of us who speak English, but just as a pun, what is Greek to you was actually Greek to the Greek! Alexander the Great developed the Greek language so that his orders would be very exacting when given to his subjects. How awesome our God is to cause this language to be developed just before the New Testament was written. Once again, to be very succinct, one verb form can make a word active or passive and change the entire paradigm of a sentence.

Once again, I would like to reiterate the fact that my Hebrew is not that of a Hebrew scholar, and so I have relied on the scholarship of *The Complete Word Study Old Testament* (AMG publishers) by Zodhiates.

Hebrew verbs operate in much the same way as discussed above. Word forms can change the paradigm of a sentence from *causative*, showing the cause of action coming from the subject, to *permissive*, showing the action of a verb coming from another cause or issue. A good example of this would be the *piel stem*. "In the piel stem, the object of a verb is passively transformed so that there is an idea of **causation**"(Notation 19, Zodhiates). When the piel stem is used in the Old Testament, it can show the cause of an action coming from another source. Perhaps a good example of this would be Jeremiah 15:7. "I will destroy" is the piel stem. The verse says, "I will destroy my people, since they do not return from their ways." Notice the cause of the destruction come from the people of God not returning from their ways. Picture a man stepping off a ten-story building. God's law of gravity is not the cause of the man's problem, is it? The cause of the man's problem is the fact that he chose to step off the building. Did God destroy that man? Did gravity destroy that man? No, the man's choice to step off the building destroyed the man! Thus, the piel stem shows the idea of the source of the causation.

Another example of word forms changing the paradigm of a sentence would be the *Hiphel stem*. "The causative sense of the hiphel stem can represent less direct ideas, such as the granting of **permission** to do a certain thing (Notation 16, Zodhiates). Deuteronomy 32:39 is an example of the hiphel stem. "I kill." Verse 30 tells us that the death which came upon those who hate Him was God surrendering them to their own rock. God granted them permission to choose their rock. Any rock other than our Rock brings death. Deuteronomy 32:31 says, "Their rock is not like our Rock."

These two stems are a basic example of how someone reading the English translation of a text might say that God was the source of the killing when He says "I kill." In actuality, people are killed all the time because they are allowed to choose life or death. God permits people to do as they will, and then He turns them over to their own way. A good New Testament example of this would be Romans 1:26, "God gave them up to." Verse 32 (NKJV) says, "who, knowing the righteous judgment of God, that those who practice such things are deserving of **death,** not only do the same but also approve of those who practice them." Now you could say God killed them, but what He does and what He permits are two different paradigms.

All of God's Word is 100 percent correct in the original manuscripts, but sometimes, because of the nuances of translation, it is possible to lose the spirit of what is actually being said by God. God made no mistakes in the words He gave to the writers of Scripture. The Scripture is not the issue. The issue is communication. Communication involves words, spirit, and gesture. Without these three elements, there are breaches in any communication. A good example of this concept would be the issue of texting which has become prevalent in the past two decades. Texting contains words but no spirit or gesture. When someone texts you, how do you know if they are happy, sad, or facetious? For example, I might text you and say "you are something else." That could mean you are special, you are an idiot, or you're from a different planet. The breach comes in spirit and gestures. If you know the person and how they have treated you in the past and other things they have said in the past, then you have a proper communication experience.

In biblical transmission (the process of copying the original manuscripts through the years), it is possible to lose the spirit of what was originally said. The biblical text we have today is a masterpiece in accuracy because of the science of textual criticism (the process of getting us the text of the original manuscripts). The issue we face today in communication deals with our hermeneutic of Scripture. To be more succinct, hermeneutics deals with the proper interpretation of Scripture. This issue is the reason so many Bible-believing Christians disagree with what the Bible is communicating. One of the scriptural laws of interpretation is the fact that the Bible does not contradict itself. For this reason, we must interpret scriptures that seem unclear by other scriptures which are clear in the rest of the Bible. Consequently, for God to say "I kill" in Deuteronomy 32:29, and then He says "I have come that they might have life" (John 10:10) and "in him is no darkness at all" (1 John 1:5) would create an issue of interpretation.

I am convinced that our concept of God affects our words, our theology, and our hermeneutic of Scripture. If we understand that biblical languages portray an accurate concept of God that must portray the proper grammatical use of words, we will always discover that the awesome Word of God never contradicts itself. Just as we know the spirit of the person who is texting us because we know the person, so it should be with God's Word. Because we know God's character from the rest of His Word and by His son Jesus, we can properly interpret His Word because we know His spirit.

I hope this brief tutorial will help you with your understanding of the next chapters.

CHAPTER 8

Hard Sayings of the Old Testament with Comparative Hebrew Grammatical Notations

In this section, I have picked out the most prominent Old Testament verses where God uses the first person singular to either kill or destroy. There are a multitude of other references where *people* say God kills or destroys. Job is a good example of this. The problem with this opinion is God says he was *wrong*!

WHO IS THIS WHO DARKENS COUNSEL BY WORDS WITHOUT KNOWLEDGE? (Job 38:2)

For this reason, I have used the first person singular references to do a comparative analysis of what God actually says He does.

Hebrew grammatical notations:

Hiphil stem:

> Is usually referred to as the causative stem. In this stem the object participates (is caused to participate) as a second subject. The stem reflects causing a state of an event or act, but is distinguished

from the Piel which often refers to causing a state to come into being. The emphasis of the stem is on the action itself, not on any state or condition that may have resulted from the action. Though in the English language the idea of causation seem always to be a matter of compulsion, the CAUSATIVE sense of the Hiphil can represent less direct ideas, such as the granting of PERMISSION to do a certain thing. (Notation 16, Zodhiates)

Qual imperfect:

Indicates, in the active voice, simple imperfect action, viewed as PART OF a whole event or situation. (Notation 95, Zodhiates)

Imperfect:

Indicates causative action, imperfect action, viewed as PART OF a whole event or situation, in the active voice. (Notation 19, Zodhiates)

Piel stem:

In the Piel stem, the object of the verb is passively transformed so that there is an IDEA of causation inherent in the meaning, though this causative is NEVER the point of emphasis. (Notation 72, Zodhiates)

Notice that all these notations are subject to part of a whole event, thus making them causative or permissive but, as with the Piel stem, is never the point of emphasis. In Hebrew, as with any language, *context* is vital to proper syntax in interpretation.

Listen to the opening comments for *grammatical notations* in Zodhiates's book.

> Furthermore it is sometimes difficult to classify properly the grammatical function of a Hebrew word. Substantively (nominal) forms from previous periods in the development of the language were by Biblical times being used as conjunctions, prepositions, and adverbs. It must be remembered that many of the grammatical terms we use are designed to identify English parts of speech and that other languages may not be limited or governed by similar definitions. In cases where certain forms of different parts of speech are identical (e.g., the verb tov, 2896), it cannot always be determined whether the word is a noun or an adjective being used in substantive construction. In each of these instances identifying the form become a matter of INTERPRETATION by the editor or translator, and this work is no exception. (2272)

1. Deuteronomy 32:39, "I kill, I make alive, I wound." Hiphil imperfect. As stated above, can represent permissive action.
2. Genesis 6:7, "I will destroy." Qal imperfect. See above. Viewed as *part of* a whole event or situation. This leaves room for causation by someone else who made a choice.
3. Jeremiah 15:7, "I will destroy." Piel perfect. See above. This causative is *never* the point of emphasis.
4. Ezekiel 25:7, "I will destroy you." Hiphil imperfect. Can represent permissive action.

Proper hermeneutic teaches us to compare scripture with scripture. Compare the above verses with Isaiah 54:16, "I have created the spoiler to DESTROY." John 10:10 (NKJV) clearly tells us who the destroyer is. "The thief does not come except to STEAL, and to KILL, and to DESTROY."

Now since we know that Jesus came to give life and not to steal, kill, or destroy, we must make a choice. Did Jesus act differently than the Father? Are He and the Father one? I believe we know the correct answer to that choice! Since the above scriptures can be translated as *causative* or *permissive*, which would you choose as to reconciling scripture with scripture? My point is, context is vital in all interpretation. If you believe in inerrancy, then the Bible cannot contradict itself.

Why Did God Strike Uzzah?

"Then the anger of the Lord was aroused against Uzzah, and God struck him there for his error; and he died there by the ark of God." To get a better context of what was behind this happening and a better understanding of what is taking place, you must look at the text.

What was the purpose of the ark? The ark had several names that are used in the Old Testament. The ark was called the ark of the covenant, the ark of the testimony, the ark of the Lord, and sometimes these names were used in conjunction with each other as in the ark of the covenant of the Lord. All of these names were used to describe a piece of furniture, or a box if you will, that was designed by God Himself to place the glory of His presence into the realm where the nation of Israel would know His presence. This was no ordinary box because in the Old Testament, God's place to meet with man was in this ark. That is why the tent that the ark was placed in was often called the tent of meeting.

The ark of the Lord was so important that its very size is described in the book of Exodus in great detail. Most scholars agree that a cubit as spoken of in the Old Testament was probably eighteen inches.

> And they shall make an ark of acacia wood; two
> and a half cubits shall be its length, a cubit and

a half its width, and a cubit and a half its height.
(Exodus 25:10)

Try to picture in your mind a box 45 inches long, 27 inches wide, and 27 inches high. It would probably be about the size of a large storage box that you might purchase at your local Walmart store, only not quite as tall. The top of this box was open and not very tall because there was another piece of furniture that was placed on top of it which we will look at in a moment. The ark was covered with pure gold in all its dimensions on the inside and outside. Four gold rings were attached to its four corners through which two gold poles were placed for carrying purposes. The priestly tribe of Kohath was commanded to carry the ark by these poles because if they were to touch the ark, they would die (Numbers 4:15).

Many people have a problem with what happened to Uzzah because after all, it says that he was just trying to steady the ark when the ox stumbled. Even David who had been worshiping and playing music before God became angry because of the Lord's outbreak against Uzzah.

> And when they came to Nachon's threshing floor, Uzzah put out his hand to the ark of God and took hold of it, for the oxen stumbled. Then the anger of the Lord was aroused against Uzzah, and God struck him there for his error; and he died there by the ark of God. And David became angry because of the Lord's outbreak against Uzzah; and he called the name of the place Perez-Uzzah to this day. (2 Samuel 6:6–8)

Both Uzzah and Ahio, who were the sons of Abinadab, were driving a new cart with the ark upon it. Ahio was in the lead, holding on to the two gold carrying poles, and Uzzah was at the rear, holding his side of the poles. When they got to the threshing floor of Nachon, there appears to have been a slight step up as you went onto the flat rock which was used to thresh grain. As the oxen stepped on this rock, the ark which was on the cart must have tilted. It seems that Uzzah decided that God needed some help, even though he knew he was not to touch the ark. When Uzzah reached out his hand and took hold of the ark, God smote him. The verb for *smote* in the Hebrew is the hiphil imperfect which, according to Hebrew grammar, can show permission or causation depending on the text.

The text says that David blamed God for His outbreak against Uzzah. The real issue is that Uzzah breached the commandment of God by touching the ark and came into direct contact with the fire of God's glory. It would appear that Uzzah fried on the spot. It is interesting that the name given to this place was Perez-Uzzah which can mean literally "outburst against Uzzah" or "Uzzah's breach." Do you suppose David was right for blaming God, or did Uzzah make the wrong choice by touching the ark? The big issue is what was the cause for this happening? To take sides with David, you would have to blame God and become angry with God as David did. This shook up David so badly that he no longer wanted the ark brought to his city. He was actually afraid of God! David then arranged to have the ark sent to the house of Obed-Edom the Gittite where he had once been in exile while running from Saul. What was he thinking? Maybe he thought God would smite them.

When the ark was in Obed-Edom, God did not smite him; instead, Obed-Edom's house was blessed because of the ark. Consequently, David finally decided to bring the ark into his city.

> Now as the ark of the Lord came into the City of David, Michal, Saul's daughter, looked through a window and saw King David leaping and whirling before the Lord; and she despised him in her heart. So they brought the ark of the Lord, and set it in its place in the midst of the tabernacle that David had erected for it. Then David offered burnt offerings and peace offerings before the Lord. (2 Samuel 6:16–17)

Uzzah's protection would have been to hang onto the golden poles which were designed to carry the ark. Listen carefully to the instructions given by God that show the purpose of these golden poles. These poles were not for aesthetics; they were put into the rings on the sides of the ark to keep the priest from touching the glory of God.

> You shall put the poles into the rings on the sides of the ark, that THE ARK MAY BE CARRIED BY THEM. The poles shall be in the rings of the ark; they shall not be taken from it. (Exodus 25:14–15)

> The sons of Kohath shall come to carry them; BUT THEY SHALL NOT TOUCH ANY HOLY THING, LEST THEY DIE. (Numbers 4:15b)

David's anger toward God came because he believed God was the cause for Uzzah's death. The real question is, did God make Uzzah take hold of the ark, or did Uzzah choose to touch the ark in spite of knowing his priestly responsibilities? When Uzzah took hold of the ark, he was choosing to ignore the written Word of God in Numbers 4:15. God, in His love for the priests, knew that they could not contact His fire without the protection of the blood of Jesus Christ. When the scripture says "God struck him," it is showing secondary causation for the cause of touching the ark! Remember, the hiphil verb form in Hebrew can show permission rather than causation.

Last Saturday, we were doing our street ministry in Statesville, North Carolina. We minister to the homeless, substance abusers, and prostitutes who have lost their dream, and many have given up on their life. One of the women we were feeding did not seem to fit in with the rest of the crowd. She was well-dressed, she had her own car, and was highly intelligent. This woman had received her bachelor's degree and had been living a very prosperous lifestyle.

I asked her if she was a child of God. She answered me and said, "Well, I used to be, but now I am mad at God and am no longer a

Christian." She went on to tell me that she thought that God had brought her the perfect husband, and they had become very wealthy in their marriage. One day, her husband left her and treacherously took all that she had. She was now homeless and mad at God because He allowed this to happen to her. Of course I explained to her that once you are a Christian, God will not let you go. When I tried to tell her that God was not her problem, she told me that He could have stopped this from happening to her. We will continue to minister to her, so pray for this woman. Her name is Sherry.

Sherry is just one example of many I have ministered to that blame God for their problems. I have had people tell me that God gave them cancer or some sickness because they did something wrong. People have told me that if God is good or even exists, He would not allow children to suffer. The false thinking of blaming God for bad things seems to be without end. People make God the cause of evil which He has not done.

The Bible says that David was mad at God, and he was afraid of God. Now after he saw that God was prospering the house of Obed-Edom, he began to realize that the presence of God was not something to be afraid of. He finally moved the ark of God into his city, and he was blessed.

The one thing many people miss when talking about the ark is the piece of furniture which covers the ark. The name for this most important item is *the mercy seat*. The mercy seat was the same length and width as the ark, and it fit perfectly on top of it. On either side of the mercy seat was a cherubim made of gold that was part of the mercy seat. The cherubim faced each other, and their wings covered the ark. It appears that cherubim in the Bible are made to guard the glory of God.

> Then the glory of the Lord went up from the cherubim and paused over the threshold of the temple; and the house was filled with the cloud, and the court was filled with the brightness of the Lord's glory. (Ezekiel 10:4)

Even though this mercy seat had the same length and width as the ark, it is very apparent that it is given no height. When I asked the Lord about this difference, He told me that it has no height because His mercies reach unto the heavens. This mercy seat shielded the high priest from the fire of God's glory which extended all the way to heaven's temple and the ark which is up there.

> Therefore it was necessary that the COPIES of the things in the heavens should be purified with these, but the heavenly things themselves with better sacrifices than these. For Christ has not entered the holy place made with hands, which are copies of the true, but into heaven itself, now to appear in the presence of God for us. (Hebrews 9:23–24)

Now the best part of this mercy seat is who it is! Yes, you read it correctly; I said who it is.

> In this is love, not that we loved God but that He loved us and sent His Son to be the PROPITIATION for our sins. (1 John 4:10)

The Greek word for *propitiation* is *hilasterion* which is translated "mercy seat" or "the lid of the ark." When you receive Jesus Christ as your Lord and Savior, you have the mercy seat inside you! You now have access to the fire of God's glory without fear of being burned up.

> Let us therefore come boldly to the throne of grace that we may obtain, MERCY and find grace to help in time of need. (Hebrews 4:16)

To conclude this subject, God did not strike Uzzah as the cause. Uzzah made a breach of God's command and faced the fire of God's glory without the protection of the finished work of Jesus Christ. My friend, you and I will one day stand in the presence of God's glory.

If you know Jesus Christ, the mercy seat, or if you will, the propitiation, you have already become a partaker of the divine nature. You will live forever in God's presence because you have the life of God (*zoe*) in you. If you do not have the life of God in you, you will burn forever in the presence of God's glory. God loves you so much that He gave part of Himself, Jesus Christ, to take your sin and to give you His righteousness. Will you come to this mercy seat right now?

Why Did God Send a Three-Day Plague at Araunah? (2 Samuel 24:1–24)

"So the Lord sent a plague upon Israel from the morning till the appointed time. From Dan to Beersheba seventy thousand men of the people died" (2 Samuel 24:15). The entire story in this text is dealing with the scriptural principal of *works versus faith*.

David, who had operated in faith against his enemies all his life, was now the king in Israel. This is David who killed Goliath with a slingshot. Remember, it was this same David who chose five smooth stones from the brook. The reason for this was because God wanted to finish off all the offspring of this giant from Gath who was a Nephilim. It appears to me that these giants, which are *Nephilim* in Hebrew, are the same class of giants mentioned in Genesis, chapter 6. These Nephilim seemed to resurface in Kadesh when Moses sent in the twelve spies to check out the promised land.

> There we saw the giants [Nephilim] (the descendants of Anak came from the giants); and we were like grasshoppers in our own sight, and so we were in our own sight. (Numbers 13:23)

The giants which were also called Anakim were also dealt with by Joshua when he took possession of the promised land.

> And at that time Joshua came and cut off the Anakim from the mountains: from Hebron, from Debir, Anab, from all the mountains of

> Judah, and from all the mountains of Israel; Joshua utterly destroyed them with their cities. None of the Anakim were left in the land of the children of Israel; they remained only in Gaza, in Gath, and in Ashdod. (Joshua 11:21–22).

We also see Caleb dealing with these giants when he took possession.

> Caleb drove out the three sons of Anak from there; Sheshai, Ahiman, and Talmai, the children of Anak. (Joshua 15:14).

We know from Joshua 11:22 that these giants remained only in Gaza, in Gath, and in Ashdod. Now fast forward to King David as a shepherd boy about seventeen years old.

> And a champion went out from the camp of the Philistines, named Goliath from **Gath,** whose height was six cubits and a span. (1 Samuel 17:4)

The story in the Bible goes on to say that David went down to the brook and chose five smooth stones and put them in his shepherd's pouch. Have you ever wondered why David chose five stones? David not only killed Goliath, but he also finished off the giant's relatives, of which there were four more.

> Then **Ish-Benob**, who was one of the sons of the giant, the weight of whose bronze spear was three hundred shekels, who was bearing a new sword, thought he could kill David. But Abishai the son of Zeruiah came to his aid, and struck the Philistine and killed him. Then the men of David swore to him, saying, "You shall go out no more with us to battle. Lest you quench the lamp of Israel." Now it happened after that there

was again a battle with the Philistines at Gob. Then Sibbechai the Hushathite killed **Saph**, who was one of the sons of the giant. Again there was war at Gob with the Philistines, where Elhanan the son of Jar-Oregim the Bethlahemite killed **the brother of Goliath** the Gittite, the shaft of whose spear was like a weaver's beam.

Yet again there was war at Gath, where there was **a man of great stature**, who had six fingers on each hand and six toes on each foot, twenty four in number; and he also was born to the giant. So when he defied Israel, Jonathan the son of Shimea, David's brother, killed him. These four were born to the giant in Gath, **and fell by the hand of David** and by the hand of his servants. (2 Samuel 21:16–22).

One might think that David who had done all these great things for God and operated in such fearless faith would never succumb to a lack of faith. The Bible says that Satan moved David to number Israel.

Now Satan stood up against Israel and moved David to number Israel. (Chronicles 21:1)

In case you did not read it in your Bible, 2 Samuel 24:1 shows a variant in the text.

Again the anger of the Lord was aroused against Israel, and He moved David against them to say, "Go, number Israel and Judah." (2 Samuel 24:1)

Those of us who believe the Bible is without error know that the Bible cannot contradict itself. So what is happening here?

The science of textual criticism is the effort of Bible-believing scholars to reproduce the *autographa* (the original inspired autographs of scripture written by the prophets). When these scholars study all the available texts, there are some variants that appear in the process of transmission. These variants, rather than detracting from the veracity of the critical text (the real autograph), actually help to pinpoint the true text of the autograph. By comparing the texts, they are able to view where the variant crept into the text. II Samuel 24:1 is an example of how a scribe capitalized the pronoun *he* and made it a *He* which would make it appear that God moved David to number Israel. The Bible tells us that God cannot be tempted with evil, nor does He tempt with evil (James 1:13). Knowing this clear teaching from the New Testament, which translation would you choose?

After David was moved by Satan to number Israel, his lack of faith displeased the Lord. Even his friend Joab tried to stop him from operating in this lack of faith, but he would not listen. Because of his mistake, he opened himself up to Satan's legal attack. Any lack of faith always opens us up to evil circumstances. God, in His justice, had a wonderful plan to thwart this situation. God gave David three choices: number one was seven years of famine, number two was to run from his enemies for three months, and number three was to face three days of plague in his land. David chose the three days of plague and threw himself on God's great mercy. There are two messianic and prophetic issues involved in how God stopped this plague.

> So the Lord sent a plague upon Israel from the morning until the appointed time. From Dan to Beershiba seventy thousand men of the people died. (2 Samuel 24:15)

The verb *sent* used here is the Hebrew qual imperfect. This verb form as shown earlier from Zodhiates's book notation 95 says "indicates in the active voice, simple imperfect action, viewed as **part of** a whole event or situation." This whole event involves David's lack of faith which opened him up to this situation. Once again, secondary causation came into effect when the Bible says "so the Lord sent."

This story deals with a prophetic view of Christ's work which began on Mount Calvary and was completed three days later at resurrection. To begin with, the very place where this event is taking place is Mount Calvary. The threshing floor of Araunah the Jebusite is where Abraham offered up Isaac as a legal transaction between him and God to reverse Adam's act of high treason. (See The Dispensation of Covenant in chapter 13.) There are many parallels that took place on Mount Calvary between Christ and Isaac.

Think about this plague at Araunah, which is also Mount Calvary. The plague which is a type of sin lasted three days. From the cross to the resurrection, Jesus dealt with the plague of sin. He became sin for us (2 Corinthians 5:21). He descended to the lower parts of the earth for three days. He came out of the grave on the third day on the same mountain and defeated the curse of death with resurrection power.

> And when the angel [messenger] stretched out his hand over Jerusalem to **destroy it**, the Lord relented from the destruction, and said to the angel who was destroying the people, "It is enough; now restrain your hand." And the angel of the Lord was by the threshing floor of Araunah the Jebusite.

Notice the two angels mentioned in this text. One angel was out to destroy; the other, the angel of the Lord, was part of the restraining process. The angel who was a destroyer was probably the same one who came as the destroyer during the first Passover (see Exodus 12:23). This was a destroying messenger who was not from God. The destroying angel is a messenger from Satan. Satan's operations always bring destruction. Consider these verses about Satan:

> Behold I have created the blacksmith who blows the coals in the fire, who brings forth an instrument for his work; and I have created the spoiler [destroyer] to destroy. (Isaiah 54:16)

> Concerning the works of men, By the word of Your lips, I have kept away from the paths of the destroyer. (Psalm 17:4)

> The thief does not come except to steal, and to kill, and to destroy. (John 10:10)

The Bible is quite clear about what Satan does. There is nothing good about him. He is a liar and the father of lies. He is a thief who is out to take your lunch and pop the bag while he is at it. When we get out of the blessings of God's *zoe* life, we move into the effect of his kingdom which always brings destruction. Satan's kingdom is the enemy of life. God's kingdom is the enemy of death. That is why we are told to choose life that we may live. Death is an enemy, and it is the last enemy that God will someday throw into the lake of fire.

> The last enemy that will be destroyed is death. (1 Corinthians 15:26)

> Then death and Hades were cast into the lake of fire. This is the second death. (Revelation 20:14)

> Nor complain as some of them also complained, and were **destroyed by the destroyer**. (1 Corinthians 10:10)

As we continue looking at some of these difficult Old Testament scriptures, it becomes strikingly apparent that they all involve the issue of choice. If God did not permit you to choose, you would be nothing more than an automaton. You would be much like a computer and would only put out what is programmed into you. Notice how many times the Bible uses the if-then construction to determine what will happen to people. Along this line, consider how many times God tells us to choose between life and death. The scriptures we are about to look at in the book of Deuteronomy is a classic example of this fact.

We all love to preach on the blessings of Deuteronomy 28:1–14. The problem comes when we miss the one little two-letter word *if.*

> Now it shall come to pass, **if** you diligently obey the voice of the Lord your God, to observe carefully all His commandments which I command you today, that the Lord your God will set you high above all nations of the earth. And all these blessings will come upon you and overtake you, because you obey the voice of the Lord your God. (Deuteronomy 28:1–2)

Life choices bring life results from God. Death choices bring death results from the destroyer. This is a spiritual principle which will always bring results.

> But it shall come to pass, **if** you do not obey the voice of the Lord your God, to observe carefully all His commandments and His statutes which I command you this day, that these curses will come upon you and overtake you. (Deuteronomy 28:15)

We live in a generation that does not comprehend consequences. Consequences, whether good or bad, come from choices. If we shelter our children from the consequences of their choices, there will be no order in their life! Absolutes are in fact the process of order. God's blessings that are stated in Deuteronomy 28:1–14 are absolutes that bring blessings from God, but when we choose to go against them, we choose to bring death upon ourselves from Satan.

Could it be that the reason the millennials of our generation think that there are no absolutes is because we have not let them face the consequences of their own wrong choices? Moral relativity says there is no right and no wrong. Consequently, when our children come up against bad *circumstances*, they blame someone else and never come to the conclusion that their problems may have been brought on by their own bad decisions. Have you ever met some-one whose reason for their bad behavior is what someone else did to them? They cannot comprehend the fact that they choose or did wrong; it is always because of someone else.

God has laid down some absolutes which are designed to keep us from making choices that open us up to the enemy's attack. Making right choices does not cause us to earn God's grace. Grace is unmer-ited. Making right choices causes us to live in the area of God's life.

> I call heaven and earth as witness today against you, that I have set before you life and death, blessing and cursing; therefore choose life that you and your descendants may **live**; that you may love the Lord your God, that you may obey His voice, and that you may cling to Him, for He is your **life** and the length of your days. (Deuteronomy 30:19–20)

Making wrong choices has the reverse effect of the blessings. The Bible refers to these things as curses. The dictionary refers to a curse as a cause for great harm or misfortune. Once again, we come to the thought-provoking question of who causes this curse. Since God does not choose for you but rather gives you permission to choose life or death, the cause would have to come from the choice made by the person or nation.

"Like a flitting sparrow, like a flying sparrow, so a curse with-out cause will not alight" (Proverbs 26:2). The language used in Deuteronomy is clearly quite graphic, and the way it is worded in the English translation makes it sound like God is the source of the destruction.

> The Lord will strike you in the knees and on the legs with severe boils which cannot be healed, and from the sole of your foot to the top of your head. (Deuteronomy 28:35)

It would be hard to get more graphic than that, but once again, the verb *strike* is in the hiphil perfect which can represent less direct ideas, such as the granting of permission to do a certain thing. Did God do it? No, He did not do it or cause it, but He did allow them to face the very destruction which they chose. It does in fact say "the Lord will strike," but the striking is a permissive action for the boils to come upon them. There are no boils in heaven, and God has no spare boils to put on them. Boils and every other form of evil and destruction come as a result of the curse of sin. These verses in Deuteronomy also demonstrate secondary causation. The primary cause is the choice being made. Consider these verses that teach this concept:

> Pronounce them guilty, oh God! Let them fall by their own counsels; Cast them out in the multitude of their transgressions, For they have rebelled against you. (Psalm 5:10)

> The Lord is known by the judgment He executes; The wicked is snared in the work of **his own hand.** Meditation. Selah. (Psalm 9:16)

It is important to notice the two words that come at the end of this verse, meditation and Selah. Both these words are injunctions given to us so that we do not just quickly blow over what is being said. God is showing us the difference between permission and causation when something is stated in the Bible.

> Let the wicked fall into their own nets, while I escape safely. (Psalm 141:10)

> The backslider in heart will be filled with his own ways, but a good man will be satisfied from above. (Proverbs 14:14)

> Concerning the works of men, by the word of your lips, I have kept from the paths of the destroyer. (Psalm 17:4)

We live in a fallen world, and good and bad things happen to both the just and the unjust. It is important to remember the fact that when I talk about permission and causation, I do not mean to imply that bad things come upon people just because they made bad choices. We must not fall into the trap that Job's friends fell into when they told Job that the things that were happening to him were a result of his bad choices. We know from Scripture that they were wrong. Satan himself was behind Job's hurt. Disease, birth defects, blindness at birth, tornadoes, hurricanes—the list is endless when describing the things we face in a messed-up world.

> Because the creation itself also will be delivered from the bondage of corruption into the glorious liberty of the children of God.
> For we know that the whole creation groans and labors with birth pangs together until now. (Romans 8:21–22)

Job's case was a result of an attack from Satan, but he is not personally the immediate cause of every issue. He is the reason for the evil, but because we live in a fallen world, things are going to happen.

My beautiful wife (the righteous fox) and I have nine children. Two of our children were born with cerebral palsy. Angel was born with this condition. She cannot use her legs, so she is in a motorized wheelchair with a joystick on the left arm of her chair because she has no use of her right arm. She has a steel rod fused into her spine because it began to curve forward when she was very young. Consequently, Angel can only lean forward with limited movement. She may appear helpless, but she has an associate's degree in psychology from Liberty University, a bachelor's degree in Christian counseling from Impact University. She has passed

NO DARKNESS AT ALL

the state of North Carolina's test for substance abuse counseling (CDAC).

We also have another daughter with the same affliction. Perla cannot use her legs or her left arm, so she is in a motorized wheelchair with a joystick on the right side for mobility. She has two bags on her abdomen because of bowel problems. This past year, Perla has been in Baptist Hospital in Winston-Salem almost as she has been at home. People might ask why did God allow this to happen to our children. What did my wife and I do to cause this to happen to our children? The answer is, we did nothing because both these daughters were adopted. Cerebral palsy came with the package. We adopted them because we loved them just as they are, with no strings attached. I mentioned this because I wanted to demonstrate that we must be very careful when we are trying to ascertain cause for any given situation. Only God can know the cause behind any given situation. Is there a cause for what has happened to them? Yes, there is a cause, but whether this issue is from their biological parents, the result of a flawed genetic because of the fall of man, or just a lack of oxygen at birth, their condition is not something God did to them. God is a good God and would never plan for the kind of suffering they have been going through.

Angel has been the Easterseals poster child in Oklahoma and twice in North Carolina. When she receives her miracle from God, no one will be able to say it was just an accident. When Perla receives her miracle, her entire family in Mexico will know God did it. To be very succinct, everything God does is good, and everything Satan does is bad. That may sound simple, but it is good theology!

The Lord struck the child that Uriah's wife bore to David, and it became ill. (2 Samuel 12:15)

Once again, we have a very difficult story where God appears to be the cause for striking David's child which was conceived in an adulterous act by King David. David was guilty of breaking more than one of God's commandments because he not only committed adultery, but he also was coconspirator in the death of her husband Uriah. Under Old Testament law, both these acts were punishable by the penalty of death. Because he had broken God's laws, David exposed his child to the attack of the destroyer. The scripture we looked at earlier in Psalm 17:4 says, "By the word of your lips I have kept away from the paths of the destroyer." The Bible says if a thief is going to break in a house, he must first bind the strongman, and then he will plunder his house (Matthew 12:29).

Here again when the Bible says "the Lord struck," the verb is in the qual imperfect where the action is viewed as part of a whole event or situation. If you were to look at this verse without looking at the whole event, it would certainly look like the Lord was the cause for this child dying some seven days later. David, like everyone else in the Old Testament, had the free will to choose from life or death choices. David made a death choice, and it opened him up to Satan taking his son. "Then on the seventh day it came to pass that the child died" (2 Samuel 12:18a). The good news is that this child went right into Abraham's bosom. David himself said, "I shall go to him, but he shall not return to me."

We know from studying David's life that even though he repented of this sin, as described in his prayer in Psalm 51, David had opened up a whole can of worms which Satan used to bring much hurt into his life. God loved David, and He was not the cause of David's hurt. David was "a man after God's own heart." David was a worshiper of God and was in the lineage of Jesus Christ. What a beautiful picture of God's grace when He even takes our failure to bring about His good!

Some Issues in the Life of Job

When you read through the book of Job, you cannot help to wonder why such destruction would come upon a man who feared God and eschewed evil. Job's life was so outstanding that he got Satan's attention. I believe the Bible shows us that Satan has his hierarchy of command just as any army would have. In Ephesians, chapter 6, we are shown this order of command when we are told that we do not wrestle against flesh and blood but against:

Principalities (*archas*)—These would be ordinary demons.
Powers (*exousias*)—demon sergeants
Rulers of the darkness of this age (*kasmokratoras*)—evil world assignments
Spiritual hosts of wickedness (*Pneumatika tes ponerias*) world rulers

Satan himself would be over all of these.

The more effective you are for God, the bigger the assignment against you becomes. Job moved all the way up the list, until he had to deal with Satan himself. Jesus Christ carried the scepter of righteousness, and He too was a target for Satan's attack. Are you and I giving Satan that kind of trouble?

The book of Job tells us that Satan approached God twice on this matter of Job. The first time, it is almost as if God is taking a jab at Satan because of Job's righteous living. I believe God enjoys it when his people are overcoming the evil that is going on all around us. God said, "Have you considered My servant Job, that there is none like him on the earth, a blameless and upright man, one who fears God and shuns evil?" (Job 1:8).

Satan said, "You built a hedge around him, his household, and all he has and I cannot touch him." We know from Scripture that one of the weapons of our warfare is the shield of faith which quenches all the fiery dart of the wicked. When you read the book of Job, it sounds like there was a time when he entered into a place of fear, and his shield of faith came down. I believe this shield of faith was the hedge Satan was talking about. "For the thing I greatly feared has come upon me, and what I dreaded has happened to me" (Job 3:25).

Notice the verb is in the past tense. *Feared* shows that this lack of faith happened before Job was opened to attack. When God said "Behold all that he has is in your power," He was saying "look, the hedge is not up any longer." At first, Satan had said to God "you touch him," but now God said to Satan "all that he has is open to you."

First of all, Satan used the Sabeans to kill his servants. Then a messenger comes and tells him a half-truth. The messenger said the fire of God fell from heaven and burned up his sheep and his servants. Fire did indeed fall on them, but it was not from God; it was from Satan. Next, Satan insisted the Chaldeans to come and raid his camels and kill his servants. Finally, a tornado comes through as a tool of Satan and kills his children.

Job's attitude toward all this was correct, but his reasoning was incorrect. Job worshiped God and said the Lord gives and the Lord takes away. God did in fact give it to him, but who took it away? Satan did.

Even after all this attack from Satan, Job continues to worship God. Job did misinterpret the things that were happening to him, but he did not stop worshiping his God. Many believers who face difficulties in their life stop worshiping God. They often hide in their own little cocoon of hurt, or they play the religious game with a facade that appears that all is well. We know that keeping an offense with people, whether we are offended or we have offended someone else, is Satan's bait to destroy us as John Bevere has so eloquently described in his excellent book *The Bait off Satan.*

Being offended with people is extremely destructive to ourselves and to them, unless reconciliation is made for healing. Because of some statements made by Job, it is quite apparent that Job was in fact offended with God.

> Know then that God has wronged me, And has
> surrounded me with His net.
>> If I cry out concerning wrong, I am not
> heard. If I cry aloud, there is no justice.
>> He has fenced up my way so that I cannot
> pass:
>> And He has set darkness in my Paths,
>> He has stripped me of my glory, and taken
> the crown from my head.

He breaks me down on every side, And I
am gone.

My hope He has uprooted like a tree. (Job
19:6–10)

That sounds like a severe case of offense to me. The point is,
you can worship God and still blame Him and be offended with
Him!

I am ashamed to say that I know this from experience. When I
was a young man, my wife of nineteen years left me for another man.
I was alone. I had four children to take care of by myself. I could
not work because I was in the hospital for three weeks with kidney
stone surgery. In my self-righteousness, I became offended with God
and had given up on the calling on my life as a pastor. I could not
understand why God would let this happen to me. I thank God that
my evangelist friend Rod McLain had a word of wisdom from God
and ministered God's love to me. I was set free, and God put me
back into the ministry. My first wife died from substance abuse com-
plications, and God gave me a wonderful wife, the righteous fox, to
whom I have been married for over thirty-five years as of this writing.

My friend, is it possible that you are holding on to a feeling
deep down that you may not even detect, feelings like God should
not have let that person hurt me, or the one I loved so much has left
me? Maybe it is one of your children who has said things that sound
so ungrateful, and maybe they have even blamed you for something
they did. How about this one; they did not see my ministry gift,
and God used someone else instead of me! Please do not become
offended with God for something He did not cause or do.

Bad things happen to the just and the unjust because of this
messed-up sin-soaked world. The goodness of God is the only answer
to this world's mess and the only thing that will change things. He
has given you and I the charge to give "grace for grace" (John 1:16)
to change things.

Are you like Job? He worshiped God but still accused Him for
his problems. Could it be that we have so stressed the sovereignty of
God beyond our free will that we have left no room for blame except

for God causing our issues? In reality, the only causing that God does is He causes all things to work out for our good. Whether your issues come from Satan, a fallen world, lack of understanding, bad theology, or your own bad choices, God is able to make them work out for your good. Thank God for His mercy!

When Satan could not stop Job the first time, he again approached God a second time, and God rubbed in Satan's failure to stop Job a little more.

> Have you considered My servant Job, that there is none like him, a blameless and upright man, one who fears God and shuns evil? And still he holds fast to his integrity, although you incited Me against him to destroy him without cause. (Job 2:3)

When you and I hang on in the middle of the storm, we frustrate Satan. He may keep on attacking like he is about to do with Job, but we still win. You can't lose with the stuff we use!

When Satan came against Job the second time, he tells God that he did not stop Job because it was about other people. He said "if **you** touch his body, he will surely curse you to your face." Why is it that most people miss the transition of action which takes place at this point? Satan said "if you touch him." God said "look, he is in your hand." Here again the hedge of protection around Job, for whatever reason, came down. Maybe Job said something stupid like "What is going to happen next. Am I going to get sick?" I know this is reading between the lines, but have we not done the same thing when trouble comes? We say things like "everything happens to me" or "If the flu is going around, I will get it." Satan is looking for an inroad to our health by using the words of our mouth.

> A man's stomach shall be satisfied from the fruit of his mouth; from the produce of his lips he shall be filled. Death and life are in the power of

the tongue, and those who love it will eat its fruit.
(Proverbs 18:20–21)

Whatever happened, we know the hedge came down, but God did not put sickness on him; Satan did it. It seems like whenever this is taught, people say that God put it on him. But what does it say?

So Satan went out from the presence of the Lord,
and struck Job with painful boils from the soul of
his foot to the crown of his head. (Job 2:7)

The opinion of people has absolutely nothing to do with what the Bible teaches. We are about to look at the opinion of Job's wife and his three friends. The Bible always speaks truth about any given situation, but what people say in Scripture is not always God's wisdom.

Have you ever considered what Job's wife was like? She was used to a rather affluent lifestyle. Remember, Job was quite well-off, and he was honored by many people. Mrs. Job probably was befriended by most of those people who were well-off in their region. When Job's affluence and dignity went out the door, we are told that his friends went in the same direction. The friends who stayed were not much help as we shall see shortly. There is little doubt that when Job's friends departed, Mrs. Job's friends went with them. The true character of a friend can only be measured by how they treat you when everything goes bad, not when you are on the top of a mountain and are waking in great prosperity.

Why did Mrs. Job marry him in the first place? It could have been an arranged marriage which was often the case in those days. It is even possible that she was a gold digger who only married Job for his possessions. Real marriage commitment is not disrupted by difficult times. Real love sticks it out no matter what the circumstances. The righteous fox and I have been through times of real need, but we hung on to our God and each other, and God always showed up. I would not trade her for anything in this world, and she feels the same way about me. By the way, you can ask her if you see her! Sonja has never told me to "curse God and die." Evidently, Mrs. Job did not feel that way about him when she made that comment. She was not only upset about her missing estate, but she wished he were dead! It is of note that she said curse God and die. Why did she not say curse Satan and die? She was very obviously in agreement with what most people thought. She believed that God did all this to Job, so she foolishly told Job to curse Him. She mockingly said, "Do you still hold on to your integrity?" She could not comprehend the fact that Job's self-worth was not based on what he had but, rather, on who his God was. What would you feel about yourself if you lost it all—your job, your money, your wife, your friends, and children? Is your identity in Christ or in your position? Job told her she was talking like one of the foolish women whoever they were.

Now let us get the opinion of Job's "friends." Someone has said, "With friends like that, who needs enemies?" Here is what Job thought about the advice of his friends: "Miserable comforters are you all! Shall words of wind have an end?" (Job 16:2). "No doubt you are the people, and wisdom will die with you" (Job 11:2).

In other words, you are all full of hot air, and you think you are the only ones who know anything. All three of Job's friends are about to unload their opinions about why all this happened to Job. Listen carefully to what they are about to say because it sounds a lot like some of the words without knowledge that are often spoken today. The Bible says that they sat down with Job for seven days and seven nights on the ground and never said a word. We shall soon see that in Job's opinion and, in fact, in God's opinion, they should have kept that posture because it would have been better for them and for Job. Someone once said it is better to be considered a fool than to open your mouth and remove all doubt!

To be fair, Job's friends were in fact very sincere in what they believed. The Bible says that they came to mourn with him and to comfort him. Job looked so pitiable to them when they saw him from a distance that they ripped their own clothes. They sprinkled dust on their own heads and sat down on the ground with him for seven days and seven nights without saying a word because his grief was so great. Try to picture this scene in your own mind. Here they sat for one hundred and sixty-eight hours in complete silence, except maybe with a lot of weeping and mourning for poor Job. Job finally broke the silence when he cursed the day he was born and said "the thing I have greatly feared has come upon me" in Job 3:25.

No one can doubt that Eliphaz, Bildad, and Zophar were very sincere in their concern for Job, but we find out later in the book of Job that God said they were perverting truth with words without knowledge (Job 38:2–3). Again the Bible always speaks truth, but not everyone speaking in the Bible is speaking truth. Satan speaks lies, and people speak lies. The point I am making is Job's friends were sincere, but they were wrong. *Sincerity and truth are not always synonymous.* This is also a very important spiritual principle. People, even good people, can be sincerely wrong. What could be more harmful than religious people deceiving someone about their eternal destiny?

I remember a religious group back in 1997 that believed heaven was coming for them on a comet called Hale-Bopp that was soon to pass near the earth. The group called their belief Heaven's Gate. Their leader was a man named Marshall Applewhite. On March 26, 1997, Applewhite told his followers their schooling was over, and now it was time to *graduate.* He actually convinced his followers to commit suicide at that time. Thirty-eight people beside himself all dressed the same, and all killed themselves so they could get to heaven which they were taught was right in the tail of Comet Hale-Bopp. All thirty-nine of their decomposed bodies were later found in one place by a police officer. The officer became so overwhelmed by the horrific odor that he had to call for help. You might say, how could all those people be deceived by such a crazy idea? Well, these people were sincere, but they were believing an untruth. Again, sincerity and truth are not always synonymous.

Job's friends are about to tell him some sincere ideas that they thought were his problem. Remember, your concept of God always affects your theology. Job's three friends' concept of God and what He does was very sincere, but it was also very wrong. It never ceases to amaze me that these same concepts are still being said by religious people today. Sometimes those of us who are in ministry are at a loss for words, and so because of ignorance, we say things that may sound godly but are in fact the opposite of God. Ignorance can often appear to be correct.

Ignorance is not always a sign of unintelligence. It can often be a lack of knowledge, or a person might just be believing what they have been taught in the past. God's Word says His people are destroyed for lack of knowledge (Hosea 4:6).

Now sometimes ignorance is in fact ignorance. I once worked construction with a young man who was one french fry short of a happy meal. Other construction workers would often pick on him because he was a bit slow. When I asked him if that kind of treatment bothered him, he said, "No, I have the gift of ignorance." Back in those days, I did not always operate in the spirit of grace, so I asked him how do you spell that? He said, "I-g-n-o-r-a-n-c-e." Of course, he meant he could ignore people, but he called himself ignorant. I am sorry, but I could not resist that story, but some people are in fact ignorant of our God. Many religious leaders today are doing nothing more than laying empty hands on empty heads because they have a misconception of God and of how He works. Now let's look at the ideas that Job's three friends are about to say through ignorance.

Eliphaz the Temanite

"Remember now, who ever perished being innocent? Or where were the upright ever cut off?" (Job 4:7). Eliphaz was telling Job, "Dude, you are guilty." Cut off was a very strong statement that probably meant God has cut you off. Remember the Bible says that the messiah would be cut off from the land of the living for the transgression of my people (Isaiah 53:8). So in a nutshell, Eliphaz was telling Job because he was in fact not innocent, God Himself was cutting him off. Was Eliphaz sincere about what he was telling Job? Yes, he was sincere, but he was not telling a truth. Sometimes in an effort to fix us, our friends speak out something that is not according to God's Word. He then goes on to describe how God supposedly did it.

"Even as I have seen, Those who plow iniquity and sow trouble reap the same. By the blast of God they perish, and by the breath of His anger they are consumed" (Job 4:8–9). Again, the Bible says very clearly in Job 2:7 "So **Satan** went out from the presence of the Lord, and struck Job." Listen again to the faulty accusations coming from the mouth of Eliphaz:

> Behold, happy is the man whom God corrects; Therefore do not despise the chastening of the Almighty. For He bruises, but He binds up; He wounds, but His hands make whole. (Job 5:17–18)

I do not mean to be redundant, but for the sake of clarity, let me ask you, who bruised Job? Who wounded Job? The text clearly states that Satan did it. When Eliphaz said do not despise the chastening of the Almighty, he is giving Job some sincere advice, but I want you to follow through with this advice. Now consider this reasoning. He is saying to Job do not despise what is happening to you but just accept it since God did it to you. Take any challenge you are facing today in your life. Let's just say you have been diagnosed with cancer, and you are feeling pretty badly about circumstances. Your pastor and all your trusted friends are telling you just accept your situation because God is doing this to you as a chastening process. You want the pain to stop, and you are sick from the chemotherapy and the radiation treatment. You cannot pray in faith to be healed because you believe God is putting this dreaded sickness on you. What is even more deceptive is the fact that you do not know that Satan is doing this to you, so you do not take the authority of Jesus's name against his attack! Someone might ask the question, How do you know I can do that? I am glad you asked that question because that is exactly what Jesus told His disciples to do when He sent them out.

> Then the seventy returned with joy, saying, "Lord even the demons are subject to us in your name."
> And He said to them, "I saw Satan fall like lightning from heaven. I give you authority [*exousia*] to trample on serpents and scorpions,

and over all the power of the enemy, and nothing
shall by any means hurt you. (Mark 10:17–19)

My question is, are you not one of His disciples? How about
this commission which He gave to *believers* just before He left the
earth?

And these signs will follow those who **believe**:
In my name they will cast out demons; they will
speak with new tongues; they will take up ser-
pents; and if they drink anything deadly, it will
by no means hurt them; they will lay hands on
the sick and they will recover. (Mark 16:17–18)

By the way, just in case you do not accept those verses just
because they are not in *Codex Sinaiticus* and *Codex Vaticanus*, try
these verses in Paul's letter to the Ephesians:

The eyes of your understanding being enlightened; that you may know what is the hope of
His calling, what are the riches of the glory of
His inheritance in the saints, and what is the
exceeding greatness of **His power toward us who
believe**, according to the working of His mighty
power. (Ephesians 1:18–19)

Now just for the record, God does chasten those of us who are
His children, but He never does it with things from Satan's kingdom.
James says, "**Let no one say** when he is tempted, 'I am tempted
by God' for God cannot be tempted by evil, nor does He Himself
tempt anyone" (James 1:13). Evil is anything in Satan's kingdom
that came about by the fall of man. So how does God correct His
children? Second Timothy 3:16 gives us the very clear answer: "All
Scripture is given by inspiration of God, and is profitable for doctrine, **for reproof, for correction,** for instruction in righteousness"
(2 Timothy 3:16).

Eliphaz goes on to say some things about Job that according to God would apply to Eliphaz more than it does to Job.

"Should a wise man answer with empty knowledge, And fill himself with the east wind?" (Job 15:2). In actuality, Eliphaz was speaking the empty knowledge and was in fact full of hot air. He takes one more shot at Job when he says: "Is it because of your fear of Him that He corrects you, and enters into judgment with you? Is not your wickedness great, and your iniquity without end" (Job 22:4–5)? How would you like a friend like Eliphaz?

Bildad the Shuhite

Now let's look at another of Job's advisers whose name is Bildad the Shuhite. Bildad begins his words against Job by trying to put a guilt trip on him. He says, "Why are we counted as beasts, and regarded as stupid in your sight? (Job 18:3). Bildad is saying, "Hey, Job, what do you think? We are stupid or something?" Because Job did not agree with his three friends, they tried to make him feel badly about it.

We need to be careful about how we treat our brothers and sisters who do not agree with us. Only God has the last word on any given issue, and His Word is always correct. It is very possible that you may be wrong, but even if you are right, you can be right and still be wrong by the way you handle your truth. Please understand that even though I am exposing God's Word as carefully as I can, I have godly brothers and sisters that are very intelligent, and I would never want to attack their belief system in a personal way as Bildad is doing in this verse. Once again, we must base our faith on the Word of God, no matter what our friends and contemporaries say.

Bildad continues his personal attack against Job by saying what has happened to him only happens to people who do not know God. "And this is the place of him who does not know God" (Job 18:2). Have you ever had a friend who told you that?

Zophar the Naamathite

Zophar the Naamathite come against Job with some of the worst criticism yet. He tells Job that God has put on him less than he deserved. "Know therefore that God exacts from you less than your iniquity deserves" (Job 11:6). Can you believe this comfort he is supposedly giving to Job? He is saying, "God should have done more than take all your possessions and kill your kids and attacked your body! Job, you deserve worse than that."

I have been a pastor for many years, and I hate to say this, but the church is the only army I know of that attacks its own soldiers when they are wounded. Zophar did to Job what many Christians now do to hurting church members. There are countless Christians who are determined to never go into a church again because of this kind of a judging spirit. Many think that God is mad at them because we have taught them that He is out to get them for what they have done.

The truth is God was not mad at Job, and what happened to him was done by Satan himself. All destruction, death, and disease come from Satan and not from God. James was dealing with this same issue in his letter to the twelve tribes that were scattered abroad from the persecution of the world. People were saying that God was tempting them with evil stuff. In other words, they were saying God puts bad things on people! James uses the imperative of positive command to rebuke them for this error. This type of command is the most powerful form of command in the Greek language. He is saying stop that. Stop saying that God is tempting or trying them with evil. The word used here is *perazomenos* in the Greek. It means tried or tempted. God does not try people with bad stuff.

> **Let no one say** when he is tempted, "I am tempted by God"; For God cannot be tempted by evil, nor does He Himself tempt anyone. (James 1:13)

This same imperative of positive command applies to us today. Are you saying things like "God killed your kids," "God caused you to lose everything," "God is making you sick"? James says "stop that; do not say that." Why would he say that? Because it simply is not true. Remember James was the half-brother of Jesus. James knew Jesus and His ministry. James knew what Jesus was like and the things Jesus would or would not do. He goes on to give another command in the same mode when he says *be not deceived.*

> Do not be deceived, my beloved brethren. Every good gift and every perfect gift is from above, and comes down from the Father of lights, with whom there is no variation or shadow of turning. (James 1:16–17)

This command was given because people were being deceived into thinking that God was not good all the time. The shadow of turning refers to the shadow of the sundial which moved with the sun. James is telling us that God does not change; He is immutable. God is always good, and He is never bad. God cannot do bad things because there is no bad thing in Him or in heaven. Where would He get the bad stuff from? He would not get it from Satan's kingdom because a kingdom divided against itself could not stand. God is always good!

Zophar finishes up his ignorance by saying that Job was not only empty-headed but also would never wise up. "For an empty-headed man will be wise, when a wild donkey's colt is born a man" (Job 11:12). Now listen to what God thought about the words that came out of the mouth of his friends.

> Who is this who darkens counsel by **words without** knowledge? (Job 38:2)

And so it was, after the Lord had spoken these words to Job, that the Lord said to Eliphaz the Temanite,

> My wrath is aroused against you and your two friends, for you have not spoken of Me what is

right, as my servant Job has; Now therefore take
for yourselves seven bulls and seven rams, go
to My servant Job, and offer up for yourselves
a burnt offering; and my servant Job shall pray
for you. For I will accept him, lest I deal with
you according to your folly; because you have not
spoken of me what is right, as my servant Job has.
(Job 42:7–8)

In chapter 42 of Job, we read about his repentance. He got his
faith sight back when he said, "I have heard you by the hearing of the
ear, but now my eye sees you." It appears that his hedge went back up
because God gave him twice as much as he had before.

Now the Lord blessed the latter days of Job more
than his beginnings; for he had fourteen thousand
sheep, six thousand camels, one thousand yoke of
oxen, one thousand female donkeys, he also had
seven sons and daughters. (Job 42:12–13)

Nadab and Abihu Are Consumed by the
Fire of God (Leviticus 10:1–3)

Aaron's two sons Nadab and Abihu decided it was a good idea
to take their father Aaron's censer and take some fire to bring into
God's presence. There are at least two issues involved in this story
that must be examined to understand why Aaron's two sons were
consumed. The first issue had to do with timing. Going before God
into the temple wherein was the ark of the covenant was an Old
Testament type of what was to take place in the prophetic future by
Jesus Christ. This was only to be done once a year at the appointed
time (*moed*). When the priest went in before the Lord, it was a con-
vocation (rehearsal) of what Jesus Christ would do at the appointed
time between the evenings (*bain haarbayim*) so that exactly at 3:00
p.m., the priest who had Aaron's censer with holy fire on it which

was taken from the altar would cut the lamb's throat and say "it is finished." This was done on Aviv the Fourteenth on Passover week.

> On the morning of the 14th at the third hour (9:00 a.m.), the lamb in the temple was bound to the altar. At the same time outside the city walls. Yeshua was both tied and nailed to a tree. For six hours both the lamb and Yeshua awaited death. At the ninth hour (3:00 p.m.). The high priest ascended the altar in the temple, took his knife, and killed the lamb, pronouncing the words "it is finished." This is the term that the priest in the temple would say with the conclusion of the daily peace offering as well as the various special festival offerings.
>
> At exactly the same moment, Yeshua on the tree gave up His spirit with the same words and died. The death of Yeshua, occurring simultaneously with that of the lamb in the temple, was no accident. (*Rosh HaShana and the Messianic Kingdom to Come*, 17)

The first issue was you cannot bring the censer into the temple just because you think it is a good idea to approach God. These events or convocations were rehearsals for the actual death of Jesus Christ. Notice what God said to Moses about the timing of what was done.

> Now the Lord spoke to Moses after the death of the two sons of Aaron, when they offered profane fire before the Lord, and died; and the Lord said to Moses: "Tell Aaron not to come **just at any time** into the Holy Place inside the veil, before the mercy seat which is on the ark, lest he die; for I will appear in the cloud above the Mercy Seat. (Leviticus 16:1–2)

The second issue is the fire they used was not from the holy fire inside the temple but was their own concoction, and God called it profane fire. Consequently, Nadab and Abihu stand before God's holy fire at the wrong time and with the wrong fire. God had warned them not to come into His presence the wrong way because they would be consumed by His glory. God cannot change what He is; He is a consuming fire. We must approach His holiness with the protection of obedience to His Word. In our dispensation, because of the blood of Christ, we are given access into His presence, but it was not so back then. God did not want them to die, but they chose to disobey His word through arrogance. Moses knew that Aaron would have a problem with this because he was a father. How would you feel if it were your children who were consumed? This is why Moses spoke to Aaron and said, "By those who come near me I must be regarded as holy; and before all the people I must be glorified" (Leviticus 10:3).

Moses went on to tell Aaron and his other sons to not even mourn over their deaths but to let the house of Israel mourn for them.

In Leviticus 10:2, when it says "fire went out from the Lord and devoured them," the word *devoured* is in the qual imperfect which shows imperfect action as viewed as part of a whole event or situation. The glory of God could not be approached under the Old Covenant because their bodies could not hold up to the fire of God's glory. Fire is always going out from the Lord because He is a consuming fire. The event or situation was that Nadab and Abihu approached that fire in an improper manner without the protection of obedience to God's instruction. Consequently, they were consumed by the fire of God's glory.

Exodus 19:18–22 is another eye-opening example of this same kind of event which would have taken place if the children of Israel were to disobey God's instructions.

Now Mount Sinai was completely in smoke because the Lord descended upon it in fire. Its smoke ascended like the smoke of a furnace, and the whole mountain quaked greatly. And when the blast of the trumpet sounded long and became louder and louder, Moses spoke, and God answered him by voice. Then the Lord came down upon Mount Sinai, on the top of the mountain. And the Lord called Moses from the top of the mountain, and Moses went up. And the Lord said to Moses, "Go down and warn the people, lest they break through to gaze at the Lord, and many of them perish. Also let the priests who come near the Lord consecrate themselves, Lest the Lord break out against them."

Thank God that under the dispensation of grace, we can now approach God without fear if we are in Christ. My friend, if you are not a child of God, your only approach to God is through the Lord Jesus Christ. If you are a child of God, Jesus Christ is your propitiation (mercy seat). You have become *fireproof* by the blood of Jesus Christ.

Singer and song writer David Ingles points this out in a song he wrote. Listen carefully to the words given in the chorus. "I am the righteousness of God in Christ / a brand-new creation in Him / I can now approach the presence of God with no condemnation of sin / I am the righteousness of God in Christ / I am now complete in Him / I am a partaker of His divine nature / on me He will not impute sin."

The Scripture tells us in Hebrews 4:16, "Let us therefore come boldly unto **the throne of grace**, that we may obtain mercy and find grace to help in time of need." Under the Old Covenant, the priest had to approach God's throne with great caution and perform the required tasks if they did not want to perish! Now we can access God directly with great boldness because His throne is a throne of *grace* for the believer in Christ.

The Strange Book of Judges

If you have given any serious study in the book of Judges, you know that it contains some of the hardest to understand stories in the Bible. The characters in this book did some very strange things, like sticking a nail through someone's head and getting a dagger stuck in a very fat man's stomach, and then you see a man cutting up his concubine into twelve pieces and sending a piece to each of the twelve tribes of Israel. People sometimes ask how a loving God would let such things happen to His people.

To answer the above issues, it is necessary to consider the time in which this book is written. Joshua, who had been leading Israel since the death of Moses, has died, and a whole generation of people who had not seen the great works of God in operation now come into the scene. Whenever any nation does not seek after God and experience His power, this same scenario takes place. What takes place in the book of Judges is not unlike what is taking place in the world today and, even more succinctly, in America. We have gotten to the place where nothing shocks us anymore. We are so desensitized to killing babies, egregious homosexuality, substance abuse, and the outright dishonesty of people scamming each other to steal what does not belong to them. These are the same four sins of the last day which it speaks about in the book of Revelation 9:21 where it says, "And they did not repent of their murders or their sorceries [*pharmikion*, drugs], or their sexual immorality, or their thefts." Recently, I was speaking to the sheriff of our community about some prank calls we have been receiving from the Social Security office about our daughter's check being canceled. They asked for her Social Security number, and fortunately, she did not give it to them. When I checked this out at the Social Security office, they said these scams are going on all the time because people are stealing citizen's numbers to access their bank accounts. Just as an aside, I hope you know that you should never give out your number to anyone unless you are at your bank or at the Social Security office yourself. They will never contact you by telephone.

The issue in the book of Judges in those days was the same philosophy that is taking place in our society. Everybody was doing what was right in their own eyes. "In those days there was no king in Israel; everyone did what was **right in their own eyes**" (Judges 21:25). My friend, that is known as *moral relativity*.

Moral relativity is what is being taught in most of our secular schools and universities. Our generation has been told that there are no absolutes to base your decisions upon; therefore, any moral choices you make should be based on what you feel is right for you or what is right in your own eyes. The problem with that kind of thinking is your decisions have consequences. Responsibility comes with consequences! Just saying there are no absolutes does not eliminate the consequences of those absolutes. The fact of the matter is to say there are no absolutes is an absolute statement which breaks down to a preconceived opinion. To teach people that there are no absolutes is to tell them there are no consequences, and whatever happens to them has nothing to do with their choices. The fact is we have raised an entire generation of children who have not been given absolutes or, if you will, boundaries. When they do something that might hurt them, instead of letting them face the consequences of their choices either by correction or pain, we have removed the consequences and shielded them from their results. As a result, they always blame their circumstances or difficulties on someone else. Our generation feels entitled for provision and sustenance no matter what they do or do not do.

The truth is, absolutes are the process of order. Where there are no absolutes, there is no order; there is confusion, pain, and disorder. In the book of Judges, they were doing what was right in their own eyes. They were living in moral relativity, and they were reaping the results of their bad choices. It was not God's will for all the evil things that were happening, but God did let them reap the results of their choices. To say that it was God's fault that all this destruction was taking place would be to say that God caused them to make the evil choices, but He did not. God allowed them to choose good and have peace, and He allowed them to choose evil and receive its results. The following stories in the book of Judges demonstrate this process:

> And the children of Israel again did evil in the
> sight of the Lord so the Lord strengthened Eglon
> king of Moab against Israel, because they had
> done evil in the sight of the Lord. (Judges 3:12)

Here again is an example of secondary causation. The cause, which is very clear in the text itself, was that Israel did evil in the sight of the Lord, so God strengthened this man called Eglon who was the king of Moab. Now this guy named Eglon made a confederacy with the people of Ammon and the people of Amalek, and they together took possession of the City of Palms. They defeated the army of Israel and kept them in slavery for eighteen years. During this eighteen-year period, a man called Euhud had to collect their tax money, and he would bring the tribute to this king called Eglon. Now here is where this story gets very strange. Eglon was a very fat man. He was not just fat, but he was what you would call excessively fat. He probably looked like one of the people on the television series called *My 600-lb Life*. He was so fat that a normal dagger could not penetrate his body. Now Euhod, who was a left-handed man, decided to finish this guy Eglon off in a very unorthodox manner. Euhod made a two-edged dagger that was eighteen inches long so it could penetrate through Eglon's fat. He went into his bedchamber to pay the tribute which he had received from the people. Now listen to what he said to Eglon, "I have a message from God for you." It would have to take a person doing what is right in his own heart to do what he is about to do. Eglon sends his servants out of the bedroom, and then Euhod reaches with his left hand and grabs the eighteen-inch dagger from his right thigh and thrusts the dagger so far into Eglon's belly that the fat rolled over his hand, so he left it in there while Eglon's entrails came gushing out. Now that was what Euhod said was his message from God.

Is it not amazing what people do even today in the name of God? Not long ago, as I was writing this thesis, a man in Florida went into a gay nightclub and began shooting people in that facility. We know that God is not in favor of gay nightclubs, but that was certainly not a message from God. One church even tried to defend the man for what he did. Doing what is right in our own eyes always brings destruction and confusion.

The above story gets even more strange when Euhod left the murder scene by locking the bedroom door and going out the back porch. When Eglon's servant came back a little later, they found his door locked, so they figured he was in the restroom relieving himself. After waiting a long time, they were embarrassed, so they went and got a key to open the door themselves. There they found Eglon, dead on the floor. You might wonder why God would allow such a story to be in the Bible. I believe God wants people to see how life would go for them if He turned them over to their own way. God, in His infinite love for us, will let us choose whatever god we choose. When people do things their way instead of God's way, these are the kinds of things that take place.

Another story in the book of Judges that follows this same kind of strangeness is the story of Jael and Sisera.

> When Euhod was dead, the children of Israel again did evil in the sight of the Lord. So the Lord sold them into the hand of Jabin, king of Canaan, who reigned in Hazor. The commander of his army was Sisera. (Judges 4:1)

Sisera, who commanded the army of Jabin the king of Canaan, was in charge of nine hundred chariots of iron. Back in those days, you not only had to finish off the army of your enemy, but you also had to put an end to the one who was in charge of that army. When his army was defeated, Sisera fled to the tent of Jael, the wife of Heber the Kenite, because he thought he would be protected by him as a friend. Now Heber's wife, whose name is Jael, wanted to finish Sisera off, so she acted like she was a friend and told Sisera to lie down in their tent. She gave him a jug of milk to drink and then she covered him with a blanket. When Sisera had fallen asleep, Jael went into the tent with a tent peg in one hand and a hammer in the other. The tent peg must have been pretty long because Jael put it to Sisera's head and drove it through his temple all the way into the ground, and that was how Sisera died. Here again you see the kind of violence that goes on when people go away from God and start doing things the way they think is right. Once again, God is not a God who causes violence, but he does permit people to choose their own way.

The question comes up once again, who did the destroying back in those days? Was God the cause of this kind of thing? He certainly was not, but when men go against God, their ways become very violent and destructive. The New Testament gives confirmation to this in 1 Corinthians 10:8–11.

> Nor let us commit sexual immorality, as some of them did, and in one day twenty-three thousand fell; nor let us tempt Christ, as some of them also tempted, and were destroyed by serpents; nor complain as some of them also complained, and were destroyed by **the destroyer.**

This verse in itself is a great commentary on what is going on in the Old Testament. The destroyer, who is none other than Satan, always brings violence and destruction into people's lives. Again, God will give people the right to choose life or death, but He tells them to choose life so that they may live.

There are many unthinkable stories that take place in the book of Judges because they were doing what was right in their own eyes, but the story of the Levite's concubine stands out in my mind as the most egregious one in the book. To begin with, a Levite was a priest of God and was supposed to be living a holy life. A concubine was a woman who was owned and used for sexual purposes outside the covenant of marriage. God does not condone this Levite's actions, but the Bible does tell us the truth about what was going on. One excellent evidence for the veracity of Scripture is the fact that it tells the truth about all its characters. Even the great heroes of the Bible were men and women who did wrong things, and the Bible tells you what they did. Books of fiction often make their characters as super-heroes who can do no wrong, but the Bible never candy coats things.

As this Levite approached the city of Gibeah during his journey, it became late, and he did not want to stay in the city of any foreigner. He wanted to stay in a city which belonged to the people of Israel. Little did he know how very wicked the people of this city were, even though they were Israelites. It sort of gets me to thinking of how wicked some so-called communities of believers has become. In our day, we even have some churches that condone and encourage gay communities. There are times when I have seen lost people live in better character than some Christians live. Unfortunately for this Levite, Gibeah had become much like the city of Sodom in Lot's day. This city had become a place where you could not even go out at night because you would be attacked by a mob of perverts. When this Levite came into the city of Gibeah, an old man saw him and asked where he was going to spend the night. The old man begged him to come to his house and not spend the night in the open square. It seems that this old man was a righteous man, and he knew what was happening at night in that wicked city. Listen to the account given in Judges 19:22–23 as to what took place as they were in this old man's house.

> As they were enjoying themselves, suddenly certain men of the city, perverted men, surrounded the house and beat on the door. They spoke to the master of the house, the old man, saying, "Bring out the man who came to your house, that we may know them carnally." (Judges 19:22–23)

By the way, the Bible is very clear about the fact that men having sex with men is perversion. No matter what people say is right in their own eyes, the Bible calls it sin. Satan is trying his best in these last days to desensitize people in their thinking so that they call it a lifestyle. It is a lifestyle, but it is a wicked lifestyle, and the Bible calls it an abomination. "You shall not lie with a male as with a woman. It is an abomination" (Leviticus 18:22). I have found out that if we even read a scripture about this to the average crowd that they accuse us of being homophobic and intolerant. Tolerance used to mean that you put up with an issue even if you do not like it. Now tolerance has come to mean you must not only accept what I do, but you must condone it. I have noticed that any nation that falls away from God and His absolutes is quickly overrun by this sin. It happened in Greece, it happened in Rome, and it is happening in our society today. I am of the opinion that the Antichrist will actually be a homosexual according to Daniel 11:37. "He shall regard neither the

God of his father nor the **desire of women**, nor regard any god; for he shall exalt himself above them all."

This event in Gibeah goes from bad to worse because even the Levite and the old man had a misconception of how to handle this situation. Once again, remember the people in those days were doing what was right in their own eyes so that even their thinking processes and moral judgment was affected by their decisions. At that time, anyone who entered your house was under your hospitality and your protection. The old man knew this, but his solution for protecting this Levite was distorted by his choices.

> But the man, the master of the house, went out to them and said to them, "No, **my brethren!** I beg you do not so wickedly! Seeing this man has come into my house, do not commit this outrage. Look, here is my virgin daughter and the man's concubine; let me bring them out now, humble them, and do with them as you please; but to this man do not do such a vile thing. (Judges 19:23–24)

I may be a bit orthodox here, but was not his suggestion just as wicked as what the men of Gibeah wanted?

These men took the Levite's concubine and abused her all night, and it seems as though the Levite did not even care. When he found her in the morning, he said, "Get up and let's go!" What a heartless attitude to have about this poor woman! When he realized she had died, the Levite took a knife, cut her into twelve parts, and sent a piece of her to each of the twelve tribes of Israel so they would come and deal with the people of Gibeah.

The Bible tells this story in detail, and many people have said what kind of a God is that in the Bible. What happens in the book of judges is not at all what our God is like. Remember these people were doing what was right in their own eyes, and God let them choose their moral condition. God has given us His moral laws because they are good and just. God's Word spells out the way for life and peace.

Every issue we have been looking at in the Old Testament deals with the permission given by God to individuals and nations. God was never the cause, nor the reason for people's destruction or death. Destruction always comes from the destroyer who is Satan.

Now that we have considered these Old Testament portions of Scripture, it is imperative that we remember the fact that the best way to properly interpret Old Testament Scripture is to compare it to New Testament teaching. The verse in 1 Corinthians 10:10 that we just looked at is a good verse to show how this principle of inter-pretation works. So let's look at this verse once more and consider what it is saying about the Old Testament event that it is referring to.

> Nor complain, as some of them also com-
> plained, and were destroyed by the **destroyer.**
> (1 Corinthians 10:10)

It is quite obvious who the destroyer is because the Scripture tells us who he is. The destroyer is in fact Satan himself who is out to "kill, steal, and destroy" (John 10:10).

The next question that logically come up is, who is the "them" that the scripture is talking about? By looking at the context, it is very apparent that it is referring to the children of Israel who had crossed the Red Sea and were now complaining about the accommodations. The story this is referring to is found in Numbers 25, but the verse I want you to consider is verse 11.

> Phinehas the son of Eleazar, the son of Aaron the
> priest, has turned back my wrath from the chil-
> dren of Israel because he was zealous with My
> zeal among them, so that I did not consume the
> Children of Israel in My zeal. (Numbers 25:11)

The verbal phrase "I did not consume" is first person singular in the piel perfect, according to the grammatical notations on page 2281, rule number 79, in Zodhiates's book *The Complete Word Study Old Testament*. Listen to the rule. "The Piel Perfect (pipf) indicates perfective achievement of a result or state, **viewed as a whole,** in the active voice." This rule of grammar makes a statement in the active voice, but the statement must be viewed as a whole. Even though it says "I did not consume" in an active sense, when viewed as a whole, you see the cause was put on the people, not God doing the action. In light of this rule, it makes perfect sense that the New Testament says in 1 Corinthians 10:10, they "were destroyed by the destroyer." Their own choices opened them up to the destroyer! So if you compare the Old Testament to the New Testament, there seems to be a contradiction. The Old Testament says God was the one consuming before the plague stopped. The New Testament says the destroyer was the one who was destroying with this plague. We know that scripture cannot contradict scripture because the Word of God is without error. So is the Old Testament correct, or is the New Testament correct? The fact is both texts are correct when viewed in light of grammatical interpretation. This same type of grammatical construct is what takes place throughout the Old Testament scriptures which we have been considering.

I know the above information gets a bit difficult to comprehend if you are not familiar with Hebrew grammar, but if you try to reason it *out*, it becomes apparent that "All scripture is given by inspiration of God, and is profitable for doctrine, for reproof, for correction, for instruction in righteousness" (1 Timothy 3:16).

CHAPTER 9

A Greek Exegesis of New Testament Scriptures

Testament Greek or Koine (common) Greek is not to be confused with Modern Greek. Koine Greek, like Latin, is no longer a spoken language. Koine Greek was developed during the time of Alexander the Great about 250 years before Christ. Greek is one of the most accurate and highly developed languages that ever existed. Word usage has highly inflected forms. Nouns have eight distinctive functions. These case functions include designation, description, separation, reception, location, means, limitation, and address. Because of the preciseness of the language, one noun, for example house, can mean the house, of the house, from the house, to the house, in the house, or with the house. It all depends on which case ending is put on the word *oikos* meaning "house." A verb in English shows time of action, but in Greek, the verb will show what kind of action is taking place also. Progressive action, completed action, and undefined act are a few examples. The above description is just a simple example of how refined the language actually is. Maybe now you can empathize with my Greek students who work so hard to learn how to parse a verb and decline a noun!

The definitive qualities of New Testament Greek have made the New Testament a valuable and highly accurate book in determining biblical doctrine. For this reason, I would like to exegete some New Testament scriptures to reinforce the proposition that God is *not* the cause behind death, destruction, and evil. While these things may cause some believers to repent, they are not caused by God to correct us. Correction, according to 2 Timothy 3:16, comes from God's Word. God does not kill babies, break legs, or put disease on people.

> This is the message which we have heard from
> him and declare to you, that God is LIGHT and in
> Him is No DARKNESS AT ALL. (1 John 1:5)

The Apostle John wrote five New Testament books and had a personal relationship with Jesus Christ while He was on the earth. John called himself the disciple whom Jesus loved. If anyone knew what Jesus was like, it was John. John watched His lifestyle. John knew what Jesus would and would not do. In short, John knew the message. So listen carefully to what he says in the above verse. "This is the message." John is about to tell us the message that Jesus told him about God the father. He also said "which we have heard." John is using the past perfect tense in the third person plural (*akakoamen*). The context is referring back to verse one where he and the other disciples had seen with their eyes. This is what they had heard Him say. Their hands had touched the results of Jesus's ministry. What was the message? "God is light." Now on the positive side, this says who or what God is. The opposite end of the spectrum is darkness. So John says "and in Him is no darkness at all." John could have said "in Him is no darkness" (*skutia en auto ouk estin*). Saying it that way would be very sufficient in the Greek to show that God has nothing to do with darkness. John does not stop with just that thought. He goes on to double negate the statement by saying "at all" (*oudemia*).

Why do you suppose he does that? Let me illustrate this. Years ago, when my son Mike was about eight years old, my "sanctification" was really put to the test. I had left some dirty oil from my truck in a five-gallon pail. Mike found the oil and an old paint brush. I think you can imagine what I am about to tell you. When I got home from work, Mike was painting our yellow rented house with the filthy black oil. I was supernaturally angry. God saved my son's hide by showing me that he was not doing it to be rebellious. He was painting the house to please me. Mike had this huge smile on his face. When Mike saw the anger on my face, he said, "Dad, are you mad?"

I said, "No, Mike, I know you are doing this because you love me, so I am not mad."

He then added, "*Not at all.*"

Do you see the point? John wants us to know there is no darkness in God; *none at all.* This is a very strong grammatical construction. It means what it says none at all—zero, zilch.

To attribute any darkness at all to God is blasphemous to the Holy Spirit. God is of a different kingdom (Matthew 12:31).

James 1:13–17

Look with me at James 1:13-17 (NKJV):

> Let no one say when he is tempted, "I am tempted by God;" for God cannot be tempted by evil, nor does He Himself tempt anyone. But each one is tempted when he is drawn away from his own desire and enticed. Then when desire has conceived, it gives birth to sin; and sin, when it is full blown, brings forth death. Do not be deceived, my beloved brethren. Every good gift and every perfect gift is from above, and comes down from the Father of lights, with whom there is no variation or shadow of turning.

James, who penned the above words under the inspiration of the Holy Spirit, is the half-brother of the Lord. James's natural mother was Mary, and Joseph was his father, according to Matthew 13:55. He is quite the troubleshooter. The abundance of commands in the book of James tells us some of the things he was shooting at. His pure Greek style is a clue to his general audience. He was addressing the Jews in Jerusalem and the Hellenistic Greek-speaking Christians who were also Jews. Like John, James knew the Lord and His teachings on a one-on-one paradigm.

The book of James is very dynamic in content. It contains 108 verses, and 54 of them are commands! James was confronting some very important issues concerning wrong things that *people were saying* and some issues that people were *deceived* by. He spoke with words of power and authority. The people respected James, so he used the Greek *imperative mood* structure in half of the 108 verses in the book. The imperative mood is very authoritative. In a very real sense, James is commanding their submission to his instructions. He is not making *suggestions*; he is issuing commands.

The imperative mood can take on different usage forms:

1. The imperative of command
2. The imperative of entreaty
3. The imperative of permission
4. The imperative of prohibition

In the text under consideration, he is using the *prohibition* form. This form is used when people are *in progress* of doing what he is commanding them *not to do*. "The present tense is properly used for expressing continued action. A prohibition in the present imperative demands that action then in progress be stopped" (Dana and Mantey, 301).

Verse 13 says, "Let no one say" (*legeto*). This is a first person singular present active imperative verb from the stem (*lego*). It shows what people were already saying. What were they saying that caused James to make this terse command? They were saying that God was *tempting them with evil*. James said, "Stop that." Do *not* say that. Quit that stuff! Why did James say that? "For God CANNOT be tempted by evil, nor does He Himself tempt anyone." He knew that God does not *cause* evil on someone to test, tempt, or try them. The word being used here is *perazomai*. It is translated "try, test, or tempt." How many times have you heard someone say, "Well, God made that awful thing happen to you to test you"? James is very emphatically saying "*No*, God does not do that." I have actually heard some people say, "God killed your baby to test your faith." *No*, He did not. "Well, pastor, God made your two daughters to be born with cerebral palsy so that they could be used for Him." *No*, He did not! If He did, then Brother James is sadly mistaken. Maybe we should inform God about James's error in interpretation! I hope you realize I am being facetious. I am simply pointing out how foolish some of our explanations are about what God does and what He does not cause.

James goes on to make another command about something that was also happening. People were deceived into thinking that God is not good all the time. They obviously thought that God was bringing evil on them to test them. Does that sound good to you? Well, it did not sound good to them either. They were being deceived. So James said, "Do not be deceived [*Me planastha*]" (James 1:16).

This form is also present imperative in the second person plural. They were already being deceived with this thinking. To contrast this, James goes on to say, "Every GOOD gift and every perfect gift is from above, and comes from the Father of Lights, with whom there is no variation or shadow of turning" (James 1:17). Back then, they had no clocks to measure time. Time was measured by the turning of the shadow on a sundial. James is telling us that God does not move from His position of *goodness*. He never has; He never will. God is immutable!

John 10:10

> The thief does not come except to steal, and to kill, and to destroy. I have come that they might have life and that they may have it more abundantly. (John 10:10)

This verse shows another great contrast between life and destruction and between Jesus and the thief. I would like to break these two contrasts down to further demonstrate my thesis. The difference between life and destruction is not difficult to describe. Moses described it quite well 3,300 years ago when he said,

> See, I have set before you today life and good, death and evil, in that I command you today to

love the Lord your God, to walk in His ways, and to keep His commandments, His statutes, and His judgments, that you may live and multiply; and the Lord your God will bless you in the land which you go to possess. But if your heart turns away so that you do not hear, and draw away, and worship other gods and serve them, I announce to you today that you shall utterly perish; you shall not prolong your days in the land which you cross over the Jordan to go in and possess. I call heaven and earth as witness today against you that I have set before you LIFE and DEATH, BLESSING and CURSING; therefore choose life that both you and your descendants may LIVE. (Deuteronomy 30:15–19)

Once again, they are two completely different forces. They are two different kingdoms that are opposed to each other. That is why Jesus came to give us the better of the two. He came to give us life and give it to us more *abundantly*. The Greek word for *abundance* is *perisos* which is translated "exceedingly, beyond measure, more, even more." It is similar to the Old Testament name for God which is El Shaddai, "more than enough." You see, God's life is *overflowing* life. Jesus said "I AM the way, the truth, and the LIFE" (John 14:6).

The second distinction in this verse is between Jesus and the thief. We know who Jesus is, but who is *the thief?* John 10:1 says, "Most assuredly, I say to you, He who does not enter the sheepfold by the door, but climbs up some other way, the same is a thief and a robber." The thief *kills*, *steals*, and *destroys*. Does that sound like God's MO to you? Now we know that God made the destroyer. "I have created the spoiler to destroy" (Isaiah 54:16).

Satan is a created being, but he was not made as the destroyer. He was made as heavens' worship leader. He was the anointed cherub who protected the glory of God.

You were the anointed cherub who covers; I established you; you were on the holy mountain of God; you walked back and forth in the midst of the fiery stones. You were perfect in all your ways from the day you were CREATED, till iniquity was found in you. (Ezekiel 28:1–15)

My friend, no matter what anyone may tell you, God is not your problem. Satan is the destroyer, and he is your problem. Someone once said "God is good *all* the time, and Satan is bad *all* the time." Jesus came to give you life. Satan is out to destroy you. They have two completely different missions. They do not mix. They cannot mix. Jesus has nothing to do with Satan's mess! My question remains the same. Since Jesus's purpose is to give life (the *zoe* of God), how could God the Father who is one with the Son cause death and destruction? (See Mark 3:24, AMP)

1 Corinthians 15:26

The last enemy that will be destroyed is death. (1 Corinthians 15:26)

I find it very important in developing my thesis that death is called an enemy. In warfare, the enemy is the opposing force. The enemy has opposing socio-political views. The enemy has a different commander. Our commander in chief is Jesus Christ. He is "Commander of the army of the Lord" (Joshua 5:14). The enemy also has a commander. He is Satan himself, the god of this world. The enemy is not the friend of God; he is just what his name portrays. He is an enemy. Why do we blame God for what the enemy does? Propaganda is a very powerful tool; it's the hands of the enemy. Satan is a master at propaganda. Do you remember what he said to Eve? It was propaganda. It was half lie and half-truth! It was designed to cause Eve to question God's motive. "Then the serpent said to the woman, 'You will not surely die. For God knows that in the day you eat of it your eyes will be open and you will be like God, knowing good and evil'" (Genesis 3:4–5). Satan was propagandizing Eve so she would think God was holding out on her. He wanted Eve to consider God as her problem. He was her enemy, not God. All he did was turn two words around and make a statement (God has said) into a question (Has God said?) His tactics have not changed much, have they? This is the point. God does not cavort with the enemy, and death is most assuredly the enemy.

Luke 6:9

> Then Jesus said to them. "I will ask you one thing: Is it lawful on the Sabbath to do good or to do evil, to save life or to destroy?" (Luke 6:9)

Here again, Jesus is calling the destruction of life *evil*. Can God commit what is evil? Absolutely not! Never! There is no evil in God. There has never been any evil in Him. God is just good. When you look at the previous verses and those which I am about to discuss, you see a pattern of New Testament teaching. Jesus Christ is against and opposite of anything that has to do with Satan and evil. Jesus hates Satan's *works* and everything that he does. Jesus never causes any of Satan's junk to come upon people.

> For the Son of Man did not come to destroy men's lives but to save them. (Luke 9:56)

Hebrews 2:14

> In as much then as the children have partaken of flesh and blood, He himself shared the same, that through death He might destroy him who HAD the power of death, that is the devil. (Hebrews 2:14)

The Greek phrase "Hina dia Tou Thanatou Katargasa" is fraught with meaning that is not readily apparent in the English translation.

Hina is more properly translated "for the purpose of, or with the result that, or in order that." The preposition *dia* is used to show agency. A more literal translation would be, "With the result of the agency of Christ's death on the cross, He might destroy him who had the [*kratos*] ruling power of death, that is, the DEVIL." The real issue I am trying to demonstrate is that Christ's work on the cross and his subsequent death was an awesome price to pay in order that the devil and ruling power would be destroyed! If Jesus did all that to stop the devil, why would he use the enemy's devices and cause death? It would be completely contrary to the purpose of the cross. It would be a contradictory act. It would in fact be treason against what Christ accomplished.

1 John 3:8

> He who sins is of the devil, for the devil has sinned from the beginning. For this purpose the Son of God was manifested, that He might destroy the works of the devil. (1 John 3:8)

The word *hina* is also used in this verse, but this time, it gives the proper context of *purpose*. The purpose of Christ being manifest was to put the devil and his works out of commission.

> And the Word became flesh and dwelt among us, and we beheld His glory, the glory as of the only begotten of the Father, full of grace and truth. (John 1:14)

If Christ was manifest for the above reason, why would God manifest anything else?

2 Corinthians 12:7

> And lest I should be exalted above measure by the abundance of revelations, a thorn in flesh

was given to me; a messenger of SATAN to buffet me, lest I should be exalted above measure. (2 Corinthians 12:7)

A great deal depends on how you translate this verse!

1. Who gave Paul this thorn in the flesh?
2. Why was it given?
3. What was the thorn in the flesh?

The obvious answer to the first question is right in the text: "A MESSENGER OF SATAN."

I never cease to be amazed at how many commentators miss that statement. It is not a messenger from God! It is from Satan. Why would Satan want to send Paul a message? He did not want Paul to pull off any more of these revelations. Paul was writing scripture, and Satan hates scripture. He fears it more than anything else. It releases God's power on him. It exposes him. It destroys his methods. God did not *cause* the thorn. God did not take away the thorn either. The thorn was given to buffet Paul. So the answer to question number two is Satan hates the Word of God.

Now we come to the big question. What was the thorn? If it was a physical affliction that God would not remove, then perhaps healing was not covered by the work of the cross. This cannot be true because of Matthew 8:16–17, which we already covered. If it was not a physical affliction that God would not remove, then what was it? The Word says, "Yes, and all who desire to live Godly in Christ Jesus will suffer persecution" (2 Timothy 3:12). The phrase "thorn in the flesh" is a Hebraism used all through the Old Testament. It is referring to a person or a group of people. Nowhere is it used to describe physical infirmity. (See Numbers 33:55 and Joshua 23:13 in chapter 4).

2 Timothy 4:20

> Erastus stayed in Corinth, but Trophimus I have
> left in Miletus SICK. (2 Timothy 4:20)

Here is another verse that people like to use to show that Paul's thorn was a physical affliction. Now even if it were a physical affliction, we have seen that God did not put it on him. Satan did that. So what's the big issue? If God allowed Paul to keep a physical affliction, then it would counter what Jesus paid for in the atonement. Healing would be for some people, but not for others. If it is not always God's will to heal you, then you cannot have positive faith to be healed. He may, or he may not. Maybe God would put sickness on you to teach you something!

So why did Paul leave Trophimus sick? Why didn't Paul lay hands on him and heal him?

Here are several possibilities:

1. The gifts of healing only operate as the Spirit wills (1 Corinthians 12:11).
2. Trophimus was a Gentile from Ephesus and may not have understood that healing was for him.
3. Maybe Trophimus, like we all do sometimes, had a lapse of faith.

The possibilities are numerous. To put this scenario on Paul to show that he too was physically sick is ridiculous!

Acts 5:1–11

> But a certain man named Ananias, with Sapphira
> his wife, sold a possession. And he kept back
> part of the proceeds, his wife also being aware
> of it, and brought a certain part and laid it at
> the apostle's feet. But Peter said, "Ananias, why
> has Satan filled your heart to lie to the Holy

Spirit and keep back part of the price of the land for yourself? While it remained, was it not your own? And after it was sold, was it not in your own control? Why have you conceived this thing in your heart? You have not lied to men but to God." Then Ananias, hearing these words, fell down and breathed his last. So great fear came upon all those who heard these things. And the young men arose and wrapped him up, and carried him out, and buried him. Now it was about three hours later when his wife came in, not knowing what had happened. And Peter answered her, "Tell me whether you sold the land for so much?" She said, "Yes, for so much." Then Peter said to her, "How is it that you have agreed together to test the Spirit of the Lord? Look, the feet of those who have buried your husband are at the door, and they will carry you out." Then immediately she fell down at his feet and breathed her last. And the young men came in and found her dead, and carrying her out, buried her by her husband. So great fear came upon all the church and upon all who heard these things. (Acts 5:1–11)

This passage does not seem to fit New Testament teaching when read superficially. We must look into the background of the context to get a clear perspective of what is taking place. It is clear that the early church had a co-op system, if you will. Those who had possessions sold them, and the apostles made an even distribution to all who had need, along with those who sold what they had. Not all the people who had possessions were required to take part in this program. It was completely voluntary. Evidently, those who chose to take part in this operation of love would get back a certain amount for their part in the program. I see several concepts in this story that must be addressed:

1. The question Peter asked Ananias
2. The preconceived plan
3. Peter's word of knowledge
4. Peter's word of wisdom

To begin with, Peter asks a question to point out where the attack against Ananias came from. What do you suppose the answer to that question is? Why did *Satan* put that in his heart? The text says that both Ananias and his wife, Sapphira, had preconceived this thing. When God's people connive to do evil, they are exposed to the lies of the devil. Their plan was to act as if they gave it all so as to take credit of the distribution from the apostles. They also kept back a secret nest egg for themselves. So Satan filled their hearts to "lie to the Holy Spirit."

If you miss why the question was asked, you will miss who had the *authority* to take their lives. *It was the devil.* The usual concept people get when reading this text is God killed them because they lied to the Holy Spirit. They did in fact lie to the Holy Spirit, but that is not what killed them! "Death and life are in the power of the tongue" (Proverbs 18:21). They exposed themselves to Satan's attack. Peter's word of knowledge from the Holy Spirit—"You have not lied to men but to God" (Acts 5:4)—showed Peter what had taken place. It was *not the cause* of Ananias's death. The same thing took place when Sapphira came on the scene. Peter got a word of wisdom from the Holy Spirit that Sapphira was about to experience the same demise. His word of wisdom did *not cause* her to die. Satan attacked her for the same reason he attacked Ananias.

When the rest of the Christians saw this happen, great respect came on them. The respect was so great that no one else wanted to join the co-op. "Yet none of the rest dared to join them, but the people esteemed them highly" (Acts 5:13).

Peter asked Ananias four questions. He asked Sapphira two. We don't know their answers, but it is clear that they were given an opportunity to answer and even repent. We know through many, many scriptures, that God's mercy would have triumphed over judgment and things would have been different for Ananias. (Pastor Murray Kartner)

Revelation 2:23

I will kill her children with death, and all the churches shall know that I am He who searches the minds and heart. And I will give each one of you according to your works. (Revelation 2:23)

There are three grammatical factors involved in giving this verse an interpretation which is hermeneutically correct.

First of all, the action of the verb *apoctaino*, "I will kill," is actually in the active voice which shows the action "will kill" comes from the pronoun *I*, referring to Christ. The verb itself is first person singular, future, active, indicative. The indicative mood confirms the reality of the action from the viewpoint of the speaker.

Secondly, the preposition used in the Greek sentence is key to understanding the active indicative use of the verb *apoctaino*. The preposition used here is *en*. Since the noun *thanato*, "death," carries the dative, lockative, or instrumental ending *oi*, it is literally translated as "by means of death." Consequently, death itself does the killing. To be more succinct, the preposition in Greek grammar helps express the verb in a more specific way.

While adverbs qualify the action, motion, or state of verbs as to manner, place, time, and extent, prepositions do also; but, in addition to this, they mark the direction and relative position of the action, motion, or state expressed by the verb. Prepositions then attend upon the verbs to help them express more specifically their relation to the substantives. (*A Manual Grammar of the Greek New Testament*, Dana and Mantey, 97)

Finally, the cause of death is by the choice made by Jezebel's children. "I give each one of you according to YOUR WORKS." Look at the following considerations:

1. The killing does not come from Christ but from the enemy which is *death*. "I have created the destroyer to destroy" (Isaiah 54:16)
2. The action is a result of the willful choice of Jezebel's children.
3. Christ turns her children over to the death they have chosen. Death is the last enemy to be destroyed. It produces the result of what it is—*death*. Another scriptural example of this is in Romans 1:24. "Therefore God gave them up to uncleanness."
4. Death never comes out of God. "In Him is no darkness at all" (1 John 1:5).

A more literal translation of Revelation 2:23 would be, "From Christ's viewpoint, HE allows the means of death [*en thanato*], the killing of her children. And all the churches shall know that I am He who searches the minds and hearts. And I give to each one of you according to your works."

CHAPTER 10

The Sovereignty of God

"The supreme rank of God as one having power and authority to rule the lives of men and creation" (Townes, 900).

The issue of God's sovereignty and man's free will has been an issue which has been hotly debated in many schools of theology. To put it more simply, some say that God predestinates man's destiny, even to the extent that He predestinates man's willful choice. Those who espouse this thinking say that God's omnipotence could not allow for man to determine his future by his own will. I believe that God is both sovereign and omnipotent, but His sovereignty has given man the right to choose. The God-given right to choose is the very issue that makes man redeemable. Satan also had a will but was not given the right to choose. Because of this, Satan is not redeemable. If God had determined for man to choose evil, that would put the cause of darkness on God because man in actuality would not have a real choice. Real choices by definition must involve the chooser's options and not be determined by the choice giver. If God had determined for Adam to make the wrong choice, it would of necessity make Him the cause of the fall and sin.

The very fact that Adam was made in God's image gave him the legal right to choose. All Satan had to do was to get him to doubt God's Word. Satan merely inverted Eve's statement "God has said" and made it into a question, "has God said?" In the English language, inverting these words turns it into a question. Satan's MO has not changed one iota. If he can get you to change your *God has said* into *has God said*, he has moved you out of faith and into doubt. Satan went on to say, "You will be like God knowing good and evil." That was only partly true. God knows good and evil, but He also knows the difference! When man fell into sin, he lost the ability to discern between good and evil. The prophet Isaiah put it like this:

> Woe to those who call evil good and good evil;
> who put darkness for light and light for darkness;
> who put bitter for sweet and sweet for bitter; Woe
> to those who are wise in their own eyes. (Isaiah 5:20–21)

You see, knowing good and evil is not the problem. Knowing the difference between the two is what has the world so messed up today. The world has inverted morality, genders, and every issue that has to do with God's wisdom. Knowing the difference between good and evil is called wisdom! To separate *light* from *darkness* is also called wisdom. Remember, this is one of the first things God did in creation. "And God saw the light and it was GOOD; and God divided the LIGHT from the DARKNESS" (Genesis 1:4).

If you do not see that there is "no darkness at all" (1 John 1:5) in God, then you do not know the difference between good and evil. Make the clear distinction! God is good all the time. Satan is bad all the time.

At the beginning of this thesis, I used the illustration of the old Quaker who was aiming and about to shoot in the direction of the barn door. His purpose was not to injure or harm the intruders who came to steal what was in the barn. This story also illustrates the sovereignty of God and the free will of man. What God is and what He does is not evil. God is a "consuming fire" (Hebrews 12:29). God's fire is His holiness. God's moral laws are an extension of who He is. God's laws are not evil; they are pure and holy because they emanate out of what He is. His commandments were designed to bring life, but without God's righteousness imputed upon us, they bring death to our mortal body. The unglorified body cannot look upon God and live. Even Moses could not look directly into God's glory.

> And he said, "Please show me your glory." Then He said, "I will make my goodness pass before you, and I will proclaim the name of the Lord before you. I will be gracious to whom I will be gracious, and I will have compassion on whom I will have compassion." But He said, "You cannot see my face; for No Man shall see me and live." And the Lord said, "Here is a place by me and you shall stand on the rock. So it shall be, while my glory passes by, Then I will take away My hand, and you shall see My backside; but My face Shall Not Be Seen." (Exodus 33:18–23)

Now since God's moral laws are part of who He is, they are also good.

> And the commandment, which was to bring Life, I found to bring Death. For sin, taking occasion by the commandment, deceived me, and It killed me. Therefore the law is holy, and the commandment is holy, and just and good. Has then what is good become death to me? Certainly not! But sin, was producing death in me through what is good, so that sin through the commandment might become exceedingly sinful. (Romans 7:10–13)

Notice the application of these verses. God and His commandment did not do the killing. Sin produced *death*, and sin did the killing. God does not want people to step into the line of fire. He gives man a freewill choice. Could it be that the fire of hell is the condition of lost people being exposed to the glory of God?

The last days are upon us, and God's wrath will be loosed in the tribulation upon all who have not received the knowledge of the truth. God's wrath is walking into His holiness without the protection of the blood of Christ.

> He who believes in the Son has everlasting life; and he who does not believe the Son shall not see life but the wrath of God abides on him. (John 3:36)

The fact is God's holiness is going to shake everything on this earth which is not under the blood of Christ. If you are a child of God, His holiness will not shake you because His holiness is in you.

> See that you do not refuse Him who speaks. For if they did not escape who refused Him who spoke on earth, much more shall we not escape if we turn away from Him who speaks from heaven, whose voice then shook the earth; but now He has promised, saying, "Yet once more I shall shake not only the earth, but also the heaven." Now this, "Yet once more," indicates the REMOVAL OF THOSE THINGS THAT ARE BEING SHAKEN, as of things that are made, that the things that CANNOT be shaken, may remain. Therefore, since we are receiving a kingdom which cannot be shaken, let us have GRACE, by which we may serve God acceptably with reverence and godly fear. For our God is a consuming FIRE. (Hebrews 12:25–29)

So how can God give us a free will if He makes all things work together for our good as *He* states in Romans 8:28? How can His sovereignty cause our freewill choice to fit into his divine plan? It almost sounds like this whole thing is rigged, does it not? Perhaps the sovereignty of God and the free will of man could be compared to the enigmas we face when trying to comprehend the Trinity, the hypostatic union, or even eternity.

The Bible talks about the Trinity and the truth that our God is one at the same time. So how can God be one and still be Father, Son, and Holy Spirit. We are taught in the Bible that they all are persons, and being persons, they have a personality. We see in the book of Ephesians, chapter 1, that the Father initiates the plan. In chapter 2 of Ephesians, the Son carries out the plan of the Father, and in chapter 3, the Holy Spirit reveals the plan of the Father. But try as we may, we must simply accept the fact that they are one. Looking through church history, it is not difficult to see all the contentions that have existed on this subject. Personally, I accept Trinitarian doctrine. The Bible speaks about all three personhoods and the fact that the Lord our God is one. Some theologians use the word *tension* when the Bible speaks about a paradox that does not fit our natural reasoning ability.

The hypostatic union is another example of what is sometimes called tension. The Bible says that Jesus Christ is all God, but at the same time, He became man at the incarnation. How could God become sin for us as it says in 2 Corinthians 5:21? If Jesus and the Father are one, as John 17:21 clearly teaches, then why did Jesus say, "My God, My God, why have you forsaken me?" in Matthew 27:46? This is the only time Jesus refers to his Father as "God."

Merriam-Webster describes tension as "either of two balancing forces causing or tending to cause tension." The question is, how far can what we know be extended in the presence of a transcendent God? After God asks some scalding questions in Job, chapters 38 and 39, He says, "Shall the one who contends with the Almighty correct Him? He who rebukes God let him answer it" (Job 40:2).

A good example of tension would be the subject of prayer in the light of a sovereign God who causes all things to fit into His divine purposes. Why should we pray if everything is already preplanned? Now at the same time, the Bible says, "The effectual, fervent prayer of a righteous man avails MUCH" (James 5:16). *Effectual* comes from the Greek word *energea* which means "released power." The English word *energy* is derived from *energea*. So how can our prayers really do something if they are already as good as done in the mind of God?

D. A. Carson states:

> It is important to see what is happening in both cases. In both instances, Christians are drawing inferences about prayer that the Bible does not draw. To put the matter another way, they are permitting one aspect or the other of the tension between divine sovereignty and human responsibility to function in ways that never occur in Scripture. In particular, they are allowing inferences drawn from one leg of the tension to destroy the other leg of the tension. One side argues that prayer brings results, it "changes things," and therefore the future cannot be totally mapped out under God's omniscience and sovereignty. God himself cannot be sovereign. The other side argues that since everything is under God's sway, and the future is already known to him, therefore our prayers must never be more than an acknowledgment his will is best. They cannot achieve anything, or make any real difference; God's will must be done in the very nature of who God is, and our prayers simply bring our wills into line with his. And thus God becomes less than personal: he no longer responds to and answers prayer. If we grant the tension between God's sovereign transcendence and his personhood, outlined in the previous chapter, is of the very essence of God's gracious self-disclosure to us in Scripture, then both of these approaches to prayer cannot possibly be right. Methodologically, they err the same way: they permit inferences drawn from one pole of the biblical presentation of God to marginalize or eliminate the other pole. What

we must ask then is what inferences the biblical writers themselves draw from each pole. How do the poles in the tension between God the transcendent and God the person function in characters in Scripture? When believers have answered that question, they should firmly resolve to make the poles of the tension function in their own prayers in the same way. In other words, compatibilism must be applied in our prayers in the same way it is applied in the prayers of Scripture.

If one views sovereignty without viewing God's legitimate granting of free will, then God indeed seems to be the primary source of evil! If one views man's free will apart from the scriptural view of sovereignty, then man appears to be the only source of his destiny! Man's free will then must be the source of secondary causation. Thus God is not the source of evil, but He does give man permission to choose between life and death. Deuteronomy 30:19 says, "I call heaven and earth as witness against you, that I have set before you life and death, blessing and cursing; therefore choose life that you and your descendants may live."

Before going any further in our discussion on the sovereignty of God and the free will of man, let me give you a working definition of two words being used by D. A. Carson in his book.

> *Tension.* When the Bible speaks a paradox of apparent opposite ideas which seem to be contradictory to our natural understanding of things.
> *Compatibilism.* The view that both the ideas which cause tension are in fact true.

The Bible as a whole, and sometimes in specific texts, presupposes or teaches that both of the following propositions are true:

1. God is absolutely sovereign, but His sovereignty never functions in such a way that human responsibility is curtailed, minimized, or mitigated.

2. Human beings are morally responsible creatures—they significantly choose, rebel, obey, believe, defy, make decisions, and so forth, and they are rightly held accountable for such actions; but this characteristic never functions so as to make God absolutely contingent (Carson, 179).

The good news is that God does not deal with good and evil in the same way. God is always the source of good things that happen (James 1:17). When God is dealing with evil, He uses secondary agents to demonstrate His justice. This does not make God any less sovereign. Secondary agency simply shows that God created Lucifer as an angel, and those who do his bidding reap the results of their own choice (Isaiah 54:16). Carson points out:

> Similarly, when the Bible speaks of God's permission of evil, there is still no escape from his sovereignty. A sovereign and omniscient God, who knows that, if he permits such and such an evil to occur it will surely occur, and then goes ahead and grants the permission, is surely decreeing the evil. But the language of permission is retained because it is part of the biblical pattern of insisting that God stands behind good and evil asymmetrically (in the sense already defined). He can never be credited with evil; he is always good. He permits evil to occur; the biblical writers would not similarly say that he simply permits good to occur! So even though permission in the hands of a transcendent and omniscient God can scarcely be different from a decree, the use of such language is part and parcel of the insistence is not merely transcendent, but that he is also personal and entirely good. That God's permission of evil does not in any way allow evil to escape the outermost bounds of sovereignty is presupposed when we are told, for instance, that the Lord per-

suades the false prophet what to say (Ezek. 14:9), or that his wrath incites David to sin by taking a census (2 Sam. 24:1). When the Chronicler describes the same incident and ascribes the effective temptation to Satan (1 Chron. 21:1), this is not in contradiction of the passage in 2 Samuel (for the biblical writers, including the Chronicler, are far too committed to allow such a view), but in complementary explanation. One can say that God sends the strong delusion, or one can say that Satan is the great deceiver: it depends on whether the sovereign transcendence of God is in view or his use of secondary agents. Some theologians are shocked by and express bitter against other theologians who speak of God "causing" evil in any sense. At one level they are to be applauded: everywhere, the Bible maintains the unfailing goodness of God. On the other hand, if you scan the texts cited in this chapter, it must be admitted that the biblical writers are rather bolder in their use of language than the timid theologians! Little is gained by being more "pious" in our use of language than the Bible is, and much may be lost. By being too protective of God, we are in fact building a grid out of only a subset of materials, and filtering out some of what is revealed in the Bible about the God who has so graciously disclosed himself. The result, rather sadly, is a god who is either less than sovereign or less than personal, either frustrated or impassive and stoical. But the God and Father of our Lord Jesus Christ is utterly transcendent and passionately personal. There are among the "givens" of Scripture and we sacrifice them to our peril. (Carson, 200)

God is sovereign, and His purposes will always be accomplished. Man has a free will that somehow always accomplishes God's purposes without controlling man's decisions. You are not an automaton. You have been appointed, anointed, and empowered to use His authority to change situations all around you. Your life can make a difference, and your prayers are God's way of releasing His energy. When God says your prayers avail much in James 5:16, he uses the adverb *effectual* in that verse. *Effectual* is the Greek word *energea* which the word *energy* or "released power" comes from in the English language. Yes, it is God's sovereign power, but God has given you authority to use it.

The sovereignty of God and the free will of man are indeed compatible, so instead of trying to reason it out, why not use your free will to choose His promises for life! Then you can watch His sovereignty go into effect to work all things out for your good.

CHAPTER 11

God's Goodness Produces Faith

In chapter 6, I spoke about the power of being convinced. Now in the light of all the things we have been examining about God being good and having no darkness at all, I know this message will produce faith in you! I would like to discuss the following reasons why the goodness of God produces faith:

1. It brings you to repentance.
2. It gives you hope.
3. It eliminates your failures.
4. It gives you back your dream.
5. It makes you fall in love with your God.
6. It convinces you that success is possible.
7. It destroys the work of your accuser.

Romans 2:4 says, "Or do you despise the riches of His goodness, forbearance, and longsuffering, not knowing that the GOODNESS of God leads you to repentance?" Many churches today seem to think that their ministry is the ministry of condemnation. Preaching guilt and condemnation is not what leads people to repentance. Trying to get people to think that God is out to get them or that God is angry with them is not our ministry. Second Corinthians 5:18 says, "Now all things are of God, who has reconciled us to Himself through Jesus Christ, and has given us the ministry of reconciliation." Knowing that God is a good God and that He is not out to get even with you will change your entire concept of God and who He is. If you think that God wants to make you sick or kill one of your loved ones because you somehow missed the mark, you will probably try to hide from God, like Adam and Eve did. On the other hand, if you believe God is a good God, you will run to Him instead of from Him. As a pastor, I have spoken to many unbelievers and even angry Christians who will not go back to church because they are angry with God, thinking that God is their problem. God is not your problem; He is your answer!

God's goodness will also give you back your hope. "For I know the thoughts that I think towards you, says the Lord, thoughts of peace and not of evil, to give you a future and a Hope" (Jeremiah 29:11). What amazes me most about this verse is the fact that God actually thinks about me. Is that not an awesome thought? God thinks about you! And what does it say He thinks? Does He say He is thinking about how badly you missed it today? Does He say "I am going to get him today and cause an auto accident because he sinned"? No, He has thoughts of peace toward you and not of evil. He desires to give you a future and a hope! Do not run away from your God. Run to Him and enjoy Him.

The goodness of God eliminates your failures. "Blessed are those whose lawless deeds are forgiven, and whose sins are covered; blessed is the man to whom the Lord will not impute sin" (Romans 4:7–8). The word *impute* is the Greek word *logizomai*. The English word *log* is derived from it. Listen to what Paul says in this verse. God will not log your sin to your account. Is that not a blessing? Your sin and my sin was logged onto Jesus Christ. He took my record and gave me His record of perfection. He did the same thing for you if you are a believer. Do you see what that does? God's goodness has eliminated your failure and given you Christ's righteousness. "For He made Him who knew no sin to be sin for us, that we might become the righteousness of God in Him" (2 Corinthians 5:21).

The goodness of God also gives you back your dream. Many men and women of God have lost their dream, their purpose, and their goal in life because they think they have outsinned God's goodness. Years ago while I was pastor, I was teaching on this subject in my church. A man began to weep at the altar call because he thought

God had given up on him. He had lost his dream and purpose in life. When he realized that God had forgiven him and wanted him in the ministry, he surrendered to God's goodness and went back into ministry. Have you lost your dream? Do you feel like it is too late? Listen to what God says:

> Through the Lord's mercies we are not consumed, because His compassions fail not. They are new every morning: Great is Your faithfulness. (Lamentations 3:22–23)

Mercy is when God does not give us what we deserve! Grace is when we get what we do not deserve! Thank God for the goodness of His grace.

God's goodness makes you fall in love with your God. "We love Him because He first loved us" (1 John 4:19). Have you ever tried to love someone who you knew did not like you? That is how some people feel about God because they think God is doing something bad to them. Back in the seventies, I had a man in my church who was a drunk. His wife was a real faith person and believed God for his salvation. One day, while he was drinking, he climbed a tree during a raging thunderstorm (not recommended). Well, he got hit by a lightning bolt and fell out of the tree. You would think that would correct him from the error of his ways, but it did not. A while later, he became drunk again during a thunderstorm, so he got under an aluminum awning at his house. You guessed it. He was again hit by a lightning bolt. He immediately got saved. This man became one of my deacons and wanted to go out soul winning. The problem was that this man did not understand that God did not send those two lightning bolts. In fact, if his wife had not been praying for him, Satan would have taken him out with lightning. Now every time we would go out soul winning, he would say to someone, "Brother Mike, tell this man he had better get saved, or God is going to kill him with a lightning bolt and send him to hell." You see, this dear brother did not understand God's love because he was convinced that God hit him with those two lightning bolts. I know this story is quite funny, but this same attitude is what keeps so many Christians from loving their God. Your attitude of how God feels about you has much to do with how you minister to people. Is it possible that people are not receiving Christ because we have misrepresented what He is really like?

The goodness of God helps you to realize that success is possible in any situation. If you were to do a careful study on the grace of God, you would discover that the root word for *grace* (*charis*) can be translated "gift, grace, or favor." You see, God wants you to succeed, so He has given you favor. What great thing would you attempt for God if you knew you could not fail? My wife and I have nine children, and it is our desire that every one of them succeed in life. Do you think that your heavenly Father wants anything less for you? One of man's greatest needs is to feel valued. Marriage relationships fall apart when one or both partners stop making the other person feel valued. When they start using phrases like "you're just like you parents" or "you never do anything right," the other person begins to feel devalued in that person's presence. How about using this phrase? "I remember what you did to me, and I will never forget it." Thank God, our God is not like that. God's goodness makes you want to be around Him, and it gives you the drive you need to succeed.

One of the greatest things about God's goodness is that it destroys the work of the Accuser. "The accuser of our brethren, who accused them before our God day and night, has been cast down" (Revelation 12:10). Just think about it. Satan has nothing left to accuse you with.

> For as far as the heavens are high above the earth,
> so great is His mercy toward those who fear Him.
> As far as the east is from the west, so far has He
> removed our transgressions from us. (Psalm
> 103:11–12)

A few years back, I was teaching on this subject in my class at Impact University. Suddenly, I heard a loud shout, and one of my students jumped up out of his chair, ran down the hall, and proceeded to start running around the school. I did not know if he was upset with something I said or if he were having a seizure of some kind. When he finally returned to the classroom, he said something like, "I am sorry, but I just got set free from my past, and I just had to start running."

God's goodness will produce faith in you and cause you to want to communicate with Him all the time. Yes, God is good all the time, and Satan is bad all the time. It's just that simple, my friend!

CHAPTER 12

Answering the Hard Questions

One of the most difficult things a pastor has to do is to answer the hard questions that his people ask him when they are going through difficult issues in life. The following list contains some of these hard questions and my answers to them which I have based on the content of this thesis.

1. Why did God let my child die?
2. Why did God allow evil in the world since it has caused so much pain and suffering?
3. How can a good God sit back and do nothing about all the awful things that happen?
4. Where was God when I needed Him?
5. Why does God not answer my prayers?
6. How could the Bible heroes do so many bad things?
7. Is there any sin that God will not forgive?
8. What is the sin unto death?
9. Why would a good God send anyone to hell?
10. What happens to babies who die?
11. When will there be peace on earth?
12. What is the lake of fire?

Why did God let my child die?

I will be answering the question of unborn babies when we get to number 10, but for now, I would like to deal with the death of children who die before their parents. No pain can compare to the pain of losing one of your children. It is like having part of who you are, part of your very being, removed. It is like having your heart removed and not dying but still feeling dead. It is like losing part of your history and part of your future all at once. Even if your child was a believer, and you know they are in heaven, the sorrow, the loss, the pain is almost unbearable. Reminders come at every familiar event, such as birthdays, the day of your loss, almost every holiday, familiar vacation spots that you spent as a family. No one can explain this kind of pain who has not experienced it firsthand.

Sonja and I were about to leave home to celebrate our twenty-fifth anniversary when we received a call that shook us to the core. One of our adult married children had died from a massive brain hemorrhage. Our immediate response was denial and unbelief. Why, God? How could you let this happen? Our faith was shaken, and we did not have any quick answers. Superficial answers given by well-meaning friends and ministers are often more painful than they are helpful. Clichés like "God needed her in heaven," "It was her time to go," "Some things just have to be left with God" or "She is in a better place" somehow fail to give much comfort. The fact is, death is an enemy. Death began at the fall of man and passed on to all mankind.

> Therefore, just as through one man sin entered
> the world, and death through sin, and thus
> death spread to all men, because all have sinned.
> (Romans 5:12 NKJV)

The question "Why did God let my child die?" is actually a question with a false assumption. The question makes a false assumption that God made my child die. That kind of a question cannot be answered with a *because* answer because it is a spurious question. The real question is, why did my child die? The enemy called death is part of what we face as a result of the fall. Man fell under a curse, and the reasons that curse takes effect on people are complex and numerous. Christ has given us His Word in order to understand how we can use

His authority to neutralize death's power. Hosea 4:6 says, "My people are destroyed for lack of knowledge." The more Word we have in us, the more we are able to use Christ's authority to counter the effects of the fall. Could we have stopped our child's death? The answer is yes. Did we stop it? The answer is no. Should we tell hurting parents that their child died because they did not know enough of God's word? The answer is absolutely not. You do not know what the factors were that caused that child to die. To impose your opinion on that kind of a situation is not only heartless and unloving; it is what the Bible calls presumption. It comes from the word *assumption*. *Presumption* is defined as assuming something before knowing the facts.

So what do I tell a grieving parent at the loss of a child? God loves you, and He loves your child. God is not the cause of your child's death. The truth is that Christ died and rose from the dead to neutralize the sting of death. Your pain is part of a grieving process that God has given you to cope with your loss. The Bible says that we do not sorrow as those who have no hope. Our hope is in Christ that we will one day be with our believing children in heaven. Will you trust God with me that He will make all things work together for our good when we are hurting? Can I pray for the peace of God to come on you right now? Pray with them and believe for the gifts of the Spirit to go into operation as you pray. God has all the answers you need!

As I was speaking to my wife about this issue, she reminded me of some of the things our daughter used to say when she would call us from another state.

Sonja said, "Honey, every time she called she would say, 'Mom, I am going to die.'"

Sonja would remind her to speak what God says about her and stop saying that.

She would answer, "But, Mom, I know I am going to die." She would say, "Mom, you do not understand. I am going to die soon."

Sonja would pray for her all the time, but she still died. Life and death really are in the power of our words. When you speak death over yourself, you are giving Satan permission to come against you. Remember, the Bible says Satan is seeking whom he *may devour*.

Now the good news is our daughter confessed Christ as her Savior, and so we know she is in heaven. We cannot help thinking how much better it would have been had she confessed this, "God's word says with long life He will satisfy me and show me His salvation (Psalm 91:16)."

Why did God allow evil to come into the world?

Since God knew that evil would come into the world and cause so much pain and suffering, why did He not stop it from happening? Would we not be much better off if evil did not exist? Well, the obvious answer is yes, things would be better without evil, but you would not exist as a person if God did not allow for choice and free will. You would be a programmed automaton, much like a computer, with a body that God programmed to do everything. You would be without personality or emotion of any kind. You could have no joy or feeling of any kind, but most of all, you could not worship God. Your worship would simply be God worshiping Himself. God would still be God over His creation, but He wanted free moral agents to worship Him and enjoy Him forever, and so He created man in His own image with a free will. Did He know man would fall into sin and cause evil? Yes, but He loved us enough to pay the price for our mess before the foundations of the world. "All who dwell on the earth will worship him, whose names have not been written in the Book of Life of the Lamb slain from the foundation of the world" (Revelation 13:8). In actuality then, God did not cause evil to come into the world. He allowed free will to come into the world with a redemptive plan to fix the mess that our free will would cause.

Every asset has a liability. Man's free will is an asset given to him by God, but free will has the liability of consequences. Our consequences are the result of our life and death choices. Every issue in life is a life or death choice. God has given us instructions for making the right choices in His Word. When we do not choose to make life choices, we experience the consequences of evil. I was sitting in church one day, and while I was listening to the message, the Lord spoke to me and said, "Take a good look at the word *live*." He caused me to see the word *live* in reverse, which happens to be *evil*. He showed me the fact that the actual letters are reciprocal in the English language. The fact is that not only are the letters opposites, but also their meanings represent two different kingdoms which are completely opposite.

Once again, the question "why did God allow evil to come into the world" is a spurious question. The real question is, why did man choose evil? The culpability then is put upon man's choice and not on God's wonderful gift of free will.

How can a good God sit back and do nothing about all the awful things that happen?

The fact is God did not just sit back and do nothing. God intervened in history and sent a Redeemer to buy back our wrong choices. Christ took on the curse of our sin so that He could fix us. Yes, even Christians face awful things, but God causes even the awful things we face to work together for our good. Since God does that for us, it is our ministry to do that for other people. At the time of this writing, there is a popular song on Christian radio called "Do Something." The songwriter asks the question to God and says, "Why don't you do something?" God says, "I did. I created you!" We who are Christians need to be the change we desire to see in the world. God has authorized, deputized, and empowered us to make that change. The truth is that everywhere the gospel of Christ goes, it relieves pain and suffering. The gospel of Christ brings hospitals, food, healthy living, and good morality wherever it goes. God is out to fix the awful things that happen.

God really does want us to do something about the awful things that are happening in this world. He has told us that we are the light of the world, and we are not supposed to hide that light under a bushel. If we as believers do nothing to fix this world's mess, then who will? One of the most rewarding things I have done in ministry was helping out at the Dream Center at Agape Faith Church. I have seen the hungry fed and clothed, but more importantly, I have seen people who had lost their dream get it back again. Many who were living on the street without a family, without shelter, and without a meaningful existence are now restored to life and purpose in Christ Jesus. They have jobs, a home, and are in fellowship at our church. Only God has the answers to the mess this world is in. There is no mess or failure that He will not fix. Job put it this way: "I know that my redeemer lives" (Job 19:25).

Where was God when I needed Him?

We have all heard the story called "Footprints." You will remember there were two sets of footprints in the sand, but then when things got bad, there was only one set of footprints. In the story, the person asks God the question "where were you then?" God answers, "It was then that I carried you!" The wonderful truth is that God never leaves or forsakes His children, but He has already taken our punishment on the cross and given us all we need for life and godliness.

> As His divine power has given to us all things that pertain to life and godliness, Through the KNOWLEDGE OF HIM who called us by glory and virtue. By which have been given to us great and precious promises, that through these you may be partakers of the divine nature, having escaped the corruption that is in the world through lust. (2 Peter 1:3–4)

God was right there when you needed Him. He was there to back up His promises with His power, but He will not do for you what He has made available to you. It is your turn to take the authority God has given you and use it to fix any situation you are in. In his book *The Believer's Authority*, Kenneth E. Hagin makes the following observation on page 7.

> Does the church of the Lord Jesus Christ have (or need) any less authority today than it had in the

first century? It would be preposterous to think so, wouldn't it? The value of our authority rests on the power that is behind that authority. God Himself is the power behind our authority! The believer who thoroughly understands that the power of God is backing him up can exercise his authority and face the enemy fearlessly. (Hagin)

Start using your authority today, and God will always be there when you need Him.

Why does God not answer my prayers?

Someone has said God always answers prayers. He says yes, no, and wait. I know that answer makes some sense, but it is an oversimplification of biblical teaching on prayer. What if you could pray the perfect prayer every time? What if you could always see your prayers answered? I have had people say to me, "Pastor, I quit praying because God did not answer my prayers." My usual reply to that statement is, what were you praying for? The answers given are invariably along the line of things that are out of priority. James 4:3 says, "You ask and do not receive, because you ask amiss, that you may spend it on your pleasures." I like to translate it this way, "you ask a mess." That may sound funny, but I actually had one man approach me when I was a young pastor with a real messed-up prayer. I had just finished preaching a message for a pastor who was on vacation. The church I preached at was a small country church in northern Illinois. Because I was young in ministry, I got to thinking how good a message I must have preached because people started coming to the altar for prayer. My ego was quickly deflated when a young man came up to me and said, "Preacher, you made me realize that I need to leave my wife because she is keeping me from going into the ministry. Would you pray for me?" I still don't remember what I preached that made him think that, but I remember telling him why I would not pray for that! If I had prayed with him for that, it would surely be asking for a mess.

Let me give you two ways to pray that will always get results: Always pray the Word of God. There is no way to pray a wrong prayer if you pray what the Word says. My beautiful wife (the righteous fox) prays the Word over our family every day. She will take a scripture and put my name in it. No weapon formed against Mike will prosper! You see, if you pray the Word of God, you are praying the perfect prayer. Another way to get results when you pray is to pray in the spirit. Jude 20 says, "But you, beloved, building yourselves up on your most holy faith, praying in the Holy Spirit." First Corinthians 14:15 says there two ways to pray. "I will pray with the SPIRIT, and I will also pray with the UNDERSTANDING." Verse 14 says when we pray with the Spirit, our spirit prays. It goes past our understanding. If you are a believer, praying in the spirit will build you up and get results.

How could the Bible heroes do so many bad things?

We are told in Hebrews 12 that we are surrounded by a great cloud of witnesses. Some see them as spectators, and some say they are examples. Whatever way you see them, the truth remains that they are being bragged on as heroes. Some of these heroes did things that we would kick them out of the fellowship for today in most churches. Noah got drunk after the flood. Abraham lied about Sarah. Sarah got rid of Hagar. Jacob was a deceiver. Moses disobeyed God and struck the rock. Rahab was a harlot. One hero after another disappoints us in godly living. How could they do such horrible things and still be heroes? The Bible does not make up fantasy people; it tells the truth about them. The truth is God takes our weaknesses and makes us into something good to honor Himself. Your biggest failures are your ministry in reverse. If God chose men and women in the Bible who were imperfect to do His ministry, then there is great potential for people like you and I.

> For you see your calling, brethren, that not many
> wise according to the flesh, not many mighty,
> not many noble, *are called*. But God has chosen

the foolish things of the world to put to shame the wise, and God has chosen the weak things of the world to put to shame the things which are mighty; and the base things of the world and the things which are despised God has chosen, and the things which are not, to bring to nothing the things that are, that no flesh should glory in His presence. (1 Corinthians 1:26–29)

The good news is that God can take your mess and make a message. Biblical examples demonstrate God's mercies to us. Sin certainly has consequences which we must deal with, and we must not let God's goodness become a license for sin. Jude, verse 4, says, "For certain men have crept in unnoticed, who long ago were marked out for condemnation, ungodly men, who turn the grace of our God into lewdness and deny the only Lord God and our Lord Jesus Christ."

If you do not believe there are sanctions for sin, just look at the heartache David went through with his children. His first son through Bathsheba died. His son Amnon violated his sister Tamar. Absalom killed his brother Amnon. Absalom committed treason against his father, David. Those are just a few of the issues David had to deal with. The Bible tells it like it is, but it also puts the consequences into perspective with Bible heroes.

Is there any sin that God will not forgive?

I am told that 80 percent of the people in mental institutes are Christians, and most of them think that they have committed the unpardonable sin. Over the course of years as a pastor, I have counseled people in this condition, and almost invariably, they think that some form of sexual sin they have committed is the reason for their state of being unforgiven. Some of the stories I have been told would probably turn you away in disgust, and so I will spare you the details. The Bible tells us there is nothing you can do to get yourself forgiven of sin apart from Christ's atonement, so why could we do something that would make us unforgiven? We are forgiven by grace.

If your sin was bigger than God's grace, that would make you greater than God's grace.

> He has not dealt with us according to our sins,
> nor punished us according to our iniquities. For
> as the heavens are high above the earth, so great
> is his mercy toward those who fear Him. As far as
> the east is from the west, so far has He removed
> our transgressions from us. (Psalm 103:10–12)

When we talk about God's forgiveness, people usually bring up the unpardonable sin that Jesus talks about in Matthew 12:31–32. This scripture actually has much to do with the content of this book.

> Therefore, I say to you every sin and blasphemy
> will be forgiven men, but the blasphemy against
> the Spirit will not be forgiven men. Anyone who
> speaks a word against the son of man, it will be
> forgiven him; but whoever speaks against the
> Holy Spirit, it will not be forgiven him, either
> in this age or in the age to come. (Matthew
> 12:31–32)

It is imperative that we know what Jesus is talking about in these two verses because of the severity of the consequences. Notice it starts out with "therefore." *Therefore* is used in Scripture to answer to the result of the previous discussion. The subject of the previous discussion is attributing Christ's miraculous power to the kingdom of Satan, rather than giving the glory to God through the Holy Spirit's power. Jesus is actually saying it is blasphemous to do such a thing when they actually saw God's glory at work in Christ. Since no one today is actually seeing Christ Himself doing things in His earthly ministry, it is not possible to do what they did. If it were possible to commit this sin today, the closest thing to it would be to accuse someone in ministry who operates in the gifts of the Spirit of doing that ministry under Satan's power.

In actuality, the only sin that cannot be forgiven today is the sin of rejecting God's wonderful plan of salvation that comes through the redemptive work of Jesus Christ. John 3:18 says, "He who believes in Him is not condemned; but he who does NOT believe is condemned already, because he has not believed in the name of the only begotten son of God." The next question I would like to discuss which people confuse with this subject is the sin unto death.

What is the sin unto death?

First John 5:16–17 says:

> If anyone sees HIS BROTHER sinning a sin which does not lead to death, he will ask, and He will give him life for those who commit sin not leading to death. There is a sin leading to death, I do not say that he should pray about that. All unrighteousness is sin, and there is a sin not leading to death.

So what is this sin that leads to death? In the first place, the word *death* used here is the Greek word *thanatos*, and it is talking about physical death. It is actually talking about a believer who is about to die because of a sin leading to death. The question is, what could this sin be? It seems to me that God, in His mercy, keeps His people from becoming reprobate by permitting them to die physically when they continue in open unrepented sin. Don't you think it would be better to die physically than to renounce Jesus Christ as your Savior and be lost forever in hell? Perhaps the sin unto death is a stopgap for the believer so that they will not get to that point. So John says "I do not say that he should pray about that." I believe some Christians die before they have to because they are exposed to death as result of sin. First Corinthians 3:15 says, "If anyone's work is burned, he will suffer loss; but he will be saved, yet so as through fire." I realize this is just a possibility for the meaning of the sin unto death, but it is as close as I can get to its meaning. Whatever the real sin unto death is, this is not talking about the unforgivable sin because the brother is still saved who commits this sin.

Why would a good God send anyone to hell?

The Bible tells us that hell was not created for people. "Then He will say to those on the left hand, 'depart from me you cursed into the everlasting fire prepared for the devil and his angels" (Matthew 25:41). God does not want anyone to go to hell, but hell is the only alternative to death outside of Christ.

> The Lord is not slack concerning His promise, as some count slackness, but is longsuffering toward us, Not willing that any should perish but that all should come to repentance. (2 Peter 3:9)

Firemen have been trained to wear the proper fire-retardant clothing to protect them when getting near a fire. They know that if they approach the fire without the covering of a fire suit, they will be overcome by the flames. The Bible says, "Our God is a consuming fire" (Hebrews 12:29). God has provided a fire suit so that we can approach His glory without fear of being consumed. His protection is the blood of Jesus Christ.

> Therefore, brethren, having boldness to enter the Holiest by the blood of Jesus, by a new and living way which He consecrated for us through the veil, that is His flesh, and having a high priest over the house of God, let us draw near with a true heart in full assurance of faith, having our hearts sprinkled from an evil conscience and our bodies washed with pure water. (Hebrews 10:19–22)

I have often wondered if hell is the condition of a person swept into the presence of a holy God without the protection of the blood of Christ. God does not send people to hell; people choose hell by not receiving God's way out. God did not create hell for mankind, but the good news is that He did create heaven for mankind to be with Him.

What happens to babies who die?

Babies who die either before birth or after birth seem to be under a special grace in the Bible because they have not yet reached the age of accountability. King David made the following statement when his baby died which he had conceived through Bathsheba. "I shall go to him but he shall not return to me" (2 Samuel 12:23). If this were not true, can you conceive of the fate of the millions of babies which have been murdered through abortion? Babies are real people at the time of conception; they are not a fetus just because you do not see them.

Back in 1990, some dear friends of mine lost their baby at birth while I was pastoring a church in Statesville, North Carolina. The Lord gave me the following words to give them.

Samantha
Daughter of Robert and Wanda Barnett
October 5, 1990

To Mom and Dad,

I heard the sounds of your words of love as I grew within your body.

Warmth and love and closeness to you is all that I ever knew.

I heard you sing to our Lord and King and the sounds of your piano.

Joy and gladness, worship and praise within you, His glory I knew.

I never knew hunger or cold or thirst for you nourished me then with your body.

One day a light appeared to me, and I was
in the arms of the Savior.

We laughed and we danced; we leaped and
we sang in the beautiful streets of glory.

When you called me back, I was given a
choice for your faith in the name of Jesus.

I could have returned, but my answer was
no, only grieve not, for this is my reason:

The Lord will come soon, and we'll meet in
the air for the rapture is right now in season.

I know you will sorrow, till I meet you
tomorrow, but see that you grieve not, nor sway.

I never knew death, only life at its best, and
life here is better each day.

If you miss me today, remember I am home,
and I know you are heading this way.

If you or a loved one have lost a baby, I pray this will minister
to you!

When will there be peace on earth?

The Greek word for *peace* is *eirene* which can be translated as
"peace, harmony, order, welfare, health" and was also used as a greeting with the word *grace* (*charis*). *Peace* would not be the right word to
describe the condition on the earth today. We live in a world of political, social, economic, and moral unrest. Words like tolerance, moral
relativity, political correctness, sexual preference, and separation of
church and state have all taken on new meanings. Our colleges and
universities are teaching our youth that there are no absolutes, and
so if it works for you, do whatever you will. This kind of thinking
teaches that boundaries are a thing of the past, and they no longer
work. People have become automatons of their own desires which
they try to quench with drugs, sexual pleasure, and things in general.
We have created the "me" generation which has caused our children

to think they are the center of the universe and the world, and their family owes them every entitlement.

Of course, none of the aforementioned will bring any of the attributes of peace. Peace is an intrinsic state. Peace has nothing to do with circumstances, bank accounts, or the strength of your portfolio. Peace can only be the result of an attitude of faith. The only truth worth having faith in is the Word of God! Peace comes by trusting a good God who is not out to hurt you but to do you good. Jeremiah 29:11 says, "For I know the thoughts that I think toward you, says the Lord, thoughts of PEACE and not of EVIL, to give you a future and a hope."

The Bible teaches us that there will never be peace on earth until Christ the righteous Judge comes in to reign on this earth. There will be false peace that will be part of the Antichrist's lie, but that will just be a deception. Jesus said in John 14:27:

> Peace I leave with you, My peace I give to you:
> not as the world gives do I give to you. Let not
> your heart be troubled, neither let it be afraid.

You can have peace on earth now right in the middle of confusion!

What is the lake of fire?

> Then Death and Hades were cast into the lake
> of fire. This is the second death. And anyone not
> found written in the Book of Life was cast into
> the lake of fire. (Revelation 20:14–15)

It would seem that hell is a temporary holding place for those who are not protected by the blood of Christ and are exposed to the fire of God's holiness. John tells us in this verse that Death, which seems to be a personification of Satan and is the last enemy to be destroyed, and Hell are cast into this final holding place called the lake of fire. My opinion is that this is also a place for those who are unredeemed, and Satan will be exposed to the glory of God.

CHAPTER 13

What About Dispensations?

The word used for *dispensation* in the Greek language is *oikonomia*. Our English word *economy* is derived from this word but is used differently. When we talk about the economy, we are usually speaking about how well our money situation is going here in the United States. However, in the New Testament, the word takes on the meaning of the stewardship of the things that transpire in the household of God. The New King James Version actually translates the word *oikonomia* as "stewardship" in 1 Corinthians 9:17 and in Colossians 1:25. The same word *oikonomia* is translated as "dispensation" in Ephesians 1:10 and 3:2.

The dispensations in the Bible have to do with God's stewardship in handling sin and man's responsibility for sin during the different time periods of biblical history. The issue of who God is and what He considers has never changed. We must remember the fact that God is an unchangeable God. Just because He handles sin differently under different biblical time periods does not change who He is. We must base our understanding of God on what the Bible says about Him. He is always good, and there is never any darkness in Him at all.

Perhaps a natural illustration would be helpful at this point. When my son Dennis was a small boy, I would give him certain responsibilities that he was accountable for, or else he would have to receive the correction necessary to bring about the repentance which was necessary for his disobedience. The purpose of the responsibility was to get my son to obey the voice of my word. You see, the correction under the economy of my house was much less difficult than the economy Dennis would have to face under the next economy in a public school or the economy of the laws of the federal government. Each succeeding economy would handle disobedience to responsibility in a different manner. A word of wisdom is appropriate at this point. If we would teach our children to obey our voice quickly the first time we say something, would it not go much easier on them when they have to keep the responsibility of their school or their job and, of course, the laws of the land? This was just a natural illustration which does not do justice to how God does things, but it does demonstrate how responsibility can change under different stewardships.

The Bible gives us information on how God handled man's sin and his responsibility for sin under seven distinct economies. These economies are usually referred to as dispensations. I would like to demonstrate at this point the seven dispensations of the Bible in order to show that God did not change what He is just because He handled sin and man's responsibility for sin in a different manner. Of the seven dispensations we are about to see, five have been historically fulfilled, and we are now living in the sixth dispensation known as the dispensation of grace. "If indeed you have heard of the dispensation of the grace of God which was given to me for you" (Ephesians 3:2 NKJV).

The dispensation of innocence

This dispensation extends from the creation of Adam until the time he was expelled from the garden. It would appear from biblical language that God recreated the earth because after Satan was cast down to the earth because of his sin, "the earth was without form, and void; and darkness was on the face of the waters" (Genesis 1:2 NKJV). (See also Ezekiel 28:12–18.) Satan always wants to destroy God's creations, but thank God He finds a way to make good out of Satan's mess.

After five days of beautiful creative work which came about by His word speaking into existence everything that Adam needed for a wonderful life, He did His creative work of the first man, Adam, on the sixth day, whom He created in His own image. Try to put yourself in Adam's place. His first conscious thought was that of God Himself breathing into him the breath of life. All his senses came alive to the freshness of his Creator's beauty. The crystalline smell of oxygen filled his nostrils. The tantalizing smells of fresh ripe fruit and the gorgeous untainted colors of the garden of Eden—all was pristine and fresh, without a hint of destruction, pain, or disease. The darkness of sin was nonexistent, and the curse of death was not to be found. No doubt God's first words to Adam were words of love and enjoyment. Because of the size of Adam's brain which was unadulterated by the knowledge of good and evil, he was able to grasp the goodness of the glory of God. In the cool of each succeeding day, they would walk, talk, and laugh together as God enjoyed him, and he enjoyed his Creator.

One beautiful afternoon, God explained to Adam his commission which was to take dominion of the earth and all that was in it. The only thing God withheld from Adam was this one lovely-looking tree with luscious-looking fruit on it. God called it the tree of the Knowledge of Good and Evil. The tree was right in the center of the garden, next to the tree of life. God told Adam that if he ate of this one tree, he would surely die. From what I understand, the words "surely die" speak of death in plurality. Man began to die physically when he disobeyed God, but even more hurtful was the fact that he died spiritually. Consequently, as a result of Adam's sin, the curse of death fell upon the entire human race.

> Therefore, just as through one man sin entered
> the world, and death through sin, and thus
> death spread to all men, because all have sinned.
> (Romans 5:12 NKJV)

After the fall, Adam began to feel fear. The Bible says he covered himself because he knew he was naked. Instead of his longing to be near God and enjoy His companionship, he wanted to run from God and hide. Things went from light to depressed darkness, from pristine beauty to the funeral procession of a twisted creation. I believe that this was the beginning of the awful pain involved in human depression. If the pain of human sickness and pain were not enough, now came a far more unbearable pain—the pain of a broken spirit. This is the pain we all feel outside of God's plan to buy us back, His plan of redemption. Adam's laughter turned into mourning. Instead of the sweet breath of God's spirit in his nostrils, all that remained was his labored breathing to just stay alive for one more breath. Adam went from communion with his creator to separation, from communication, which is the process of life, to confusion. For Adam's own sake, God even closed him off from the beautiful garden, and He moved the tree of life into heaven for further use in His plan of salvation. The dispensation of innocence began with God's provision and ended with man's failure. The good news is that God had a plan in mind to deal with Adam's sin. Adam turned in his religion of fig-leaf covering for God's covering of animal skins made by a blood sacrifice. God also left Adam with the good news that the enemy would one day be bruised by the seed of a woman, and his head would be bruised even though he would bruise the heel of His only Son (see Genesis 3:15).

The dispensation of conscience

As we have seen earlier in this thesis, Satan was not completely wrong when he told Eve that she would be like God knowing good and evil. The problem was not just knowing good and evil. The real issue was knowing the difference. Remember we said earlier that it takes God's wisdom to know the difference. The big issue which still exists in modern society is that the natural man calls good evil and evil good. We now face the issue of moral relativity which says good and evil are based on your opinion instead of God's absolutes of wisdom. Under the dispensation of conscience, man had to now make a moral choice to do good and eschew evil. Man was now responsible to make the right moral choice.

Correct moral choices cannot be made without a correct absolute because it is the correct absolute which determines what is good and what is evil. I have a friend who is a college professor in our state. If you were to ask him what absolute truth is, he would tell you that there are no absolutes because all truth must be based on what you feel is good or what you feel is not good. This philosophy was also going on in the book of Judges where "everyone did that which was right in their own eyes" (Judges 17:6). If you were to press this professor about the certainty of his philosophy that there are no absolutes, he would say he was *absolutely* sure that there are no absolutes! You see, without a standard for what is good and what is evil, you have no axiom with which you can determine truth. For someone to say there is absolutely no truth, that statement within itself becomes an axiom. The irony of this kind of reasoning is more clearly seen when someone says it is not fair for a loving God to allow pain and suffering. The problem is fairness itself says that there has to be an absolute to determine what is fair and what is not fair. Absolutes are in fact the process of order, and absolutes must be based on truth because veracity is the process of reality.

Back in the 1980s, I was a concrete foreman for a company which was building a sewage treatment plant. My responsibility was to determine the proper grades for the aerobic digester which was being installed to handle the incoming sewage for the city of Statesville, North Carolina. I will spare you the details of the purpose of this container of raw sewage. Before I could shoot the grades for any part of the digester, I had to determine the benchmark for the sea level of this area of Statesville. A benchmark is determined by the army corp of engineers that tells you the distance above sea level at any given point. A benchmark is an absolute that you must use to determine correctness when shooting grades. The benchmark at this particular sight in Statesville is 828 feet above sea level. I would set my leveling instrument at this benchmark and shoot all the necessary grades on the blueprint from the absolute grade of 828 feet above sea level. I am sure I did it correctly because when people flush their toilets in Statesville the water goes downhill! I use this illustration to point out the importance of an absolute. What would have happened if I were to start with a benchmark that I felt was correct? I am sure the entire system would have ended in failure. The dispensation of conscience ended in complete failure because man lost the moral capacity to distinguish between good and evil.

The condition of things at the end of this time period which we are calling conscience has a disturbing similarity to the condition of the world we now live in. The Bible says in Genesis 6:5, "Then the Lord saw that the wickedness of man was great in the earth and that every intent of the thoughts of his heart was only evil continually." Matthew 24:37 tells us, "But as the days of Noah were so will be the coming of the son of man."

Secondary causation once again comes into effect. Because of the choices man was making, God was about to send a flood which would destroy every living thing that could not swim. The wickedness of man made the intents of the thoughts of his heart unable to choose the salvation of the grace of the ark. "But Noah found grace in the eyes of the Lord" (Genesis 6:8). Evidently, Noah was the only one who, at the end of this dispensation, was able to discern good from evil. He was the only one who had the wisdom to build an ark for the saving of his household.

> By faith Noah, being divinely warned of things not yet seen, moved with godly fear, prepared an ark for the saving of his household, by which he condemned the world and became heir of the righteousness which is according to faith. (Hebrews 11:7)

The Greek word used here for *household* is actually the same stem word which is used for *dispensation*. It was Noah's faith that caused him and his family to not be destroyed by the flood.

It seems almost ironic that the very thing which is used in the Bible to bring life is the cause of death to those who followed after evil. Jesus himself said that He was the water of life.

> But whoever drinks of the water that I shall give him will never thirst. But the water that I shall

give him will become in him a fountain of water
springing up into everlasting life. (John 4:14)

We also see that the sign of the covenant that God made was the rainbow. He said He would never again destroy the earth with a flood. We now understand that a rainbow is actually water vapor which is being refracted by light. Have you ever considered the fact that the Hebrew word for *covenant* which is *bereeth* actually means "a cutting"? Light from the sun actually cuts water vapor into the colors of the spectrum. When Moses wrote the book of Genesis under inspiration of the Holy Spirit, science had not yet proved that the rainbow was "cut light." God knew what it did because it was part of His creation. Consequently, the rainbow was in fact covenant or cutting of water vapor. What an awesome God we have!

It also seems significant that the generation we live in has taken the sign of the covenant, the rainbow, and flaunted the sin of homosexuality in God's face by using the rainbow as a banner for their transgression of His precepts. How merciful our God is to continue to reach out in grace in our dispensation so we can reach out in love to bring lost people to Christ. It is God's goodness that leads people to repentance!

God ended the dispensation of conscience by dividing Noah's three sons Shem, Ham, and Japeth into separate nations, and He gave them some important instructions about human government. He told them not to eat flesh with its blood in it (Genesis 9:4–5). He also gave human government the use of capital punishment as a deterrent to man's wickedness. The Bible says that God told his sons to be fruitful and multiply and to populate the then known earth as they divided into various parts of world.

The dispensation of human government

It appears that under the dispensation of human government, one of the sons of Ham, whose name was Cush, had a son named Nimrod. Now Nimrod seems to have been a very charismatic person and became famous because of his ability to hunt. Nimrod started a kingdom called Babel which was in the land of Shinar. Shinar is probably modern-day Iran. By reading between the lines, you will see that Nimrod somehow became so influential that he brought all the nations together under one-world government. We read at the end of Genesis, chapter 10, in verse 31 and 32, that the nations had been divided by location and by languages into various parts of the earth.

Genesis 11:1 says that somehow the whole earth was of one language and one speech. How do you suppose that happened? I personally believe that Nimrod was a type of the Antichrist. Nimrod established the Babylonian system whereby the world came under one language, one world power, one world economy, one world religion. Is that not what the Antichrist system which is already at work is bringing us into today? God Himself said "now nothing that they propose to do will be withheld from them" (Genesis 11:6). This same Babylonian system will be reestablished by the Antichrist himself at the end of the age, and Christ will put a stop to it in Revelation 17 where religious Babylon comes down and Revelation 18 when political Babylon is taken down.

Human government cannot bring world peace, nor can it solve the world's problems. It ended in failure back then as God, in His mercy, put an end to it, and it will end in failure in our dispensation when Christ comes to put a stop to the lie of the Antichrist. In all this, God did not change who He was, nor did He operate under Satan's kingdom to put a stop to man's failure to properly govern himself. After the failure of human government, God was about to set up a new economy which would eventually set up a *Seed* for the future dispensation of grace.

The dispensation of covenant or promise

Before we talk about the dispensation of covenant or what is sometimes referred to as the dispensation of promise, I feel like it is imperative to understand some issues about God's attributes.

God cannot lie! This may seem like a very obvious issue, except for the fact that we live in a society where prevarication or, if you will, stretching the truth or not speaking the whole truth and nothing but the truth has become an acceptable way of life. In time past, a man's word was a part of his character. A handshake of agreement was as good or even better than a legal contract because you did not need to hire a lawyer to see that it was carried out. The old Indian expression for a lie was to "speak with a forked tongue." God never speaks with a forked tongue because He is one with His word. God is what He says, and what He says He is. In fact, He says that He honors His word above His Name. When God makes a promise, we can say amen, which means so be it, because His Word is a state of being!

God is always good. Someone has said if it's not good, it's not God. The goodness of God in the Bible is equated to His glory. In the book of Exodus, Moses asked God to show him His glory. In response, God said to Moses, "I will make all my goodness pass before you" (Exodus 33:19). Could it be possible that the reason we do not experience the glory of God as we need to is because we have blamed God for that which is not good? For example, death is not good, but God is always good. Sickness is not good, but God is always good. Destruction is not good, but God is always good. Breaking your leg is not good, but God is always good. Am I making my point? The goodness of God is synonymous with the glory of God; the two are inseparable.

God is always just; His justice is part of who He is. Consequently, He cannot do anything that is unjust. What I am about to say is my personal opinion, and I know some will disagree with this thinking. I believe that God could not legally or, if you will, justly redeem mankind from the curse of Adam's sin without dealing with Adam's high treason against Himself. When Adam sold out his God-given dominion to Satan at the fall, God had to redeem mankind in a way that was in keeping with His Justice. It is my opinion that God was looking for three things that were necessary to operate in His justice.

First of all, God needed a man who was born under Adam's race. God needed a man whose seed would produce two sets of descendants. Abraham's natural descendants would be the nation of Israel whom He was going to use to bless the entire human race. Abraham's natural descendants would possess the land of Palestine.

> On the same day the Lord made a covenant with Abram, saying, "To your descendants I have given this land, from the river of Egypt to the great river, the River Euphrates." (Genesis 15:18)

Abraham's spiritual descendants were his other set of descendants. These descendants were not seeds as of many but a seed.

> Now to Abraham and his Seed were the promises made. He does not say, "and to seeds," as of many, but as of one, "and to your Seed," who is Christ. (Galatians 3:16)

Abraham's spiritual descendants came through Isaac who, as we shall see, was part of God's legal plan to redeem the human race.

Secondly, God needed a man who was in covenant with Him. In those days, covenant was a very serious contract. People in covenant with each other would basically be saying anything that is mine is yours, and anything that is yours is mine. Your need is my need, and my need is your need. Abraham believed God and entered into covenant with Him. The Scriptures tell us that because Abraham believed God, it was accounted to him for righteousness. The Scriptures preached the gospel to Abraham *beforehand* according to Galatians 3:8.

Lastly, God needed a man who was willing in covenant to do with His only begotten Son exactly what He was willing to do with His only begotten son. Perhaps God spoke the gospel to Abraham beforehand and said, "Abram, I am going to send my only begotten Son to Mount Moriah (Mount Moriah is the threshing floor of Araunah which is Mount Calvary [see 2 Samuel 24, 1 Chronicles 21, and 2 Chronicles 3:1]) and offer Him up for a sacrifice for sin.

Consider the parallels in the account in Genesis 22 where Abraham offers up his only begotten son:

Jesus had a supernatural birth.	Isaac had a supernatural birth.
Jesus carried the cross up Mount Moriah.	Isaac carried the wood up Mount Moriah.
God was willing to give His son.	Abraham was willing to give his son.
Jesus was the lamb.	Abraham was provided a lamb (Genesis 22:8).
Jesus was laid on the wooden cross.	Isaac was laid on an altar of wood.
God got him back on the third day.	Abraham got him back on the third day (Genesis 22:4).

The legal transaction was completed between God and Abraham. Abraham has natural descendants, the nation of Israel, perhaps the sand of the sea. Abraham has spiritual descendants, perhaps the stars of heaven (see Genesis 22:17). "And if you are Christ's then you are Abraham's seed, and heirs according to the promise" (Galatians 3:29).

We know that Abraham's natural descendants disbelieved God. When famine came, they left the promised land and went to Egypt where God had planted Joseph to provide for them as they grew and multiplied. Abraham's descendants eventually came under hard slavery under the pharaoh of Egypt. Sadly, the book of Genesis which opened with the words "in the beginning God" ends with the words "in a coffin in Egypt."

The dispensation of the law

With the natural descendants of Abraham in bondage in Egypt, God would now raise up a deliver named Moses. In the New Testament, those who were under the law were under Moses's house, and the church which is under grace is called Christ's house.

> And as Moses indeed was faithful in all His house as a servant, for a testimony of those things which would be spoken afterward, but Christ as a son over His own house, whose house we are if we hold fast the confidence and the rejoicing of the hope firm to the end. (Hebrews 3:5–6)

There is a difference of opinion as to whether the *His* which is capitalized in the New King James Version is a pronoun referring to God as the antecedent or to Moses. Either way, the Bible refers to Christ's house as having more honor.

Much of the legalistic preaching we hear today may sound spiritual and holy because the law is in fact good and holy. The problem is that the law made nothing perfect (see Hebrews 7:19). An even harder pill to swallow is the truth that the law comes with the curse of having to keep the whole law all the time.

> For as many as are of the works of the law are under the curse; for it is written, "Cursed is everyone who does not continue in all things which are written in the book of the law, to do them." (Galatians 3:10)

Those who try to justify what God did under the law say that He did certain things in the Old Testament differently, and so it was fine for God to kill people under the law. God has never changed His righteous requirements of the law. God was showing people that they could not keep His righteous laws. The law was a schoolmaster to lead us to His grace.

When the people heard the law, instead of crying out for God's grace with an attitude of repentance for all they had done, they brashly proclaimed "All that the Lord has spoken we will do?" (Exodus 19:8). The legalistic religious boasting of many has not changed very much in our generation. When doing good becomes a standard for righteousness, its proponents have put themselves back under the dispensation of the law and have put themselves under its curse! Legalistic churches put people under an unattainable goal, leading them to a place of failure, guilt, condemnation, and defeat. The legalistic drop-outs usually wind up in worse sin than the unsaved or in mental institutions thinking they have committed the unpardonable sin.

When the children of Israel came to Kadesh Barnea, they did not operate under a spirit of faith because they were trying to see the situation by what they could do instead of what God was promising them. The giants of self-righteousness are just as big as the Anakim that they were facing. Self-righteousness always leads people into the wilderness of failure. Self-righteousness ultimately led Israel into idolatry, even in the promise land where the nation was divided and went into slavery. The dispensation of the law ended in failure, not because the law of God was evil but because Israel reaped the second-ary causation of destruction by not operating in faith.

God, in His mercy and grace, ended the Old Covenant with this promise which would be fulfilled some four hundreds later. "But to you who fear my name The Sun of righteousness shall arise With healing in His wings" (Malachi 4:2).

The dispensation of grace

Before we consider the dispensation of grace it is imperative to reemphasize that the God of the New Covenant is the same God as the God of the Old Covenant. Not long ago, my daughter Angel and I were watching a movie called the *Pink Panther*, starring Steve Martin. In one of the scenes in this comedy, Steve Martin, Inspector Clouseau, does the good-cop-bad-cop routine which is used in police interrogation to get people to confess to a crime. I am sure you have seen this done in any detective movie. One cop comes into the inter-rogation room, and he is the bad guy who treats the suspect with tough warnings and bad behavior. He causes the suspect to get all frustrated and angry with him so that the person being interrogated does not even want to speak with him at all. The bad cop figure then walks out, and in comes the good cop who treats the suspect with congeniality and respect. The philosophy is of course to get the suspect to think he is his friend who is getting him to confess to the same crime. The routine will often work, but it must be done with two different cops. In the movie, Inspector Clouseau enters the room as the bad cop creating the animosity that is needed to anger the suspect. He then reenters the room as the good cop who is entirely different, with all kinds of congeniality and good will. The punch line comes when his partner, who is privy to the routine, says to him, "I think you are supposed to use two different cops."

The illustration I am making is that this is exactly what some theologians have done with God's character. One must either make the God of the Old Testament a different God than the God of the New Testament, as the theologian named Marcian did, or you would have to say that the God of the Old Testament was the same person who was doing the good-cop-bad-cop routine. Of course, neither of the two stated above are correct. God has always been the God of grace, and He will always be the God of grace.

The Greek word for *grace*, which is transliterated as *charis*, can be translated as "grace, favor, or gift," depending on the context of the verse. Whatever way it is used, it always shows something being given which is undeserved or unmerited. Grace is often used in conjunction with God's mercy which does not give us what we do deserve or have merited. In the fullness of time, under the new covenant, God makes full payment for the grace which was provided under the old covenant by the down payment of animal blood sacrifice. God's goodness was always His goodness, and His grace was always His grace. It always has been and it will always be accessed by faith. "For by grace you have been saved by faith" (Ephesians 2:8). Think of it as you would think about being a homeowner. The bank takes a down payment knowing that the entire mortgage will be amortized at the appointed time. At the closing, you then move into the house and become a homeowner. Under the new covenant, or dispensation of grace, God Himself amortizes the mortgage and pays it off once for all through Jesus Christ!

> He takes away the first that He may establish
> the second. By that will [covenant] we have been

> sanctified through the offering of the body of
> Jesus Christ once for all. (Hebrews 10:9–10)

In our dispensation of grace, God is now giving believers His righteousness instead of requiring their righteousness.

> For they being ignorant of God's righteousness,
> and seeking to establish their own righteousness,
> have not submitted to the righteousness of God.
> For Christ is the end of the law for righteousness
> to everyone who believes. (Romans 10:3–4)

The dispensation of the fullness of time

It would appear that the dispensation of the fullness of time begins when Christ comes for His church.

> That in the dispensation of the fullness of time
> He might gather together in one all things in
> Christ, both which are in heaven and which are
> on earth—in Him. (Ephesians 1:10)

This dispensation is also called the dispensation of the kingdom under the Davidic covenant. According to Scripture, Jesus Christ will reign on the throne of David for one thousand years which we call the millennial reign of Christ. Before the reign of Christ, there will be a period of seven years when the wrath of God will be loosed on the earth.

The wrath of God is not a change of who God is, nor does it make Him the author of destruction. The wrath of God is in fact the glory of God being confronted by those who have not entered into God's rest by faith. Human wrath is usually an outburst of anger that is vengeful and seeks to even the score with someone who we feel has wronged us. We express our wrath with either angry words or physical attack which is brought on by an unforgiving attitude. We make plans in our minds for ways to make the person hurt by whom we have been offended. Human wrath and an unforgiving attitude hurts us and causes us to react in a way that affects our character. To be more succinct, it alters our personality so that we change into something that looks rather ugly.

The wrath of God has nothing in common with human wrath. Since God is unchangeable, He is always what He is, and what He is does not get affected by what people do or do not do. The wrath of God is how you are affected by what He is! The wrath of God is the glory of God.

> The temple was filled with smoke from THE GLORY OF GOD and from His power and no one was able to enter the temple till the seven plagues of the seven angels were completed. Then I heard a loud voice from the temple saying to the seven angels, "Go and pour out the bowls of the wrath of God on the earth." (Revelation 15:8–16)

When this happened, the mark of the beast on the people affected by this glory turned into a foul, loathsome sore. That mark which is probably a badge of honor to the unbelieving masses now becomes exposed for what it really is, a loathsome sore. Whenever darkness is turned into the light, it is exposed for what it is. Nothing can stand the glory of a holy God that is not covered by the blood sacrifice of His holy Son, Jesus. Jesus is the cleft in the rock whereby God covers us with His hand to shield us from His glory. To the child of God, His glory brings life. To the child of wrath, our God who is a consuming fire becomes their kindling point of eternal destruction. Could it be that hellfire is everything outside of Christ being exposed to the glory of God without the protection of His grace? Remember, the mercy seat in the temple was a covering for the glory of God that was inside the arc of the covenant. Without the mercy seat, the high priest would wind up being a piece of charcoal and would have to be pulled out from under the veil of the Holiest of Holies. The Greek word for mercy seat is *hilesterion* which is translated "propitiation." Just in case you have missed the point, Jesus Christ is the mercy seat;

He is our propitiation. It is He who gives us privilege to stand in the presence of the glory of God in our glorified bodies in heaven after the rapture. It is Christ, our propitiation, who has positioned us with Him right now at the throne of grace in heaven. "Let us therefore come boldly to the throne of grace, that we may obtain mercy and find grace to help in time of need" (Hebrews 4:16).

Throughout all past dispensations and through the dispensation to come, God is always good, and His goodness is unchangeable. Remember also that God equated His goodness to His glory. Both the goodness of God and the glory of God are inseparable.

CONCLUSION

I know the book I have presented will be disputed. I have personal friends who are well-respected ministers that would counter what I have said. As I have said, there are scriptures that appear to teach that God puts death and sickness on people. I respect the opinions of my peers and would never attack their ministry.

I believe the weight of evidence from the clear passages of Scripture about God's character demand a proper hermeneutic to interpret the passages which seem to teach otherwise. There are multiple possibilities in the Hebrew grammar and syntax that would at least allow for my thesis.

A good thesis is considered to be the result of original research. When I began research on this thesis, I felt in my heart that the findings would line up with what I believe the Bible teaches about God's goodness and that He is in fact separate from any form of evil. To be candid, I did not know what my research would reveal about my conviction. I did make up my mind that whatever the result was, my heart must be subject to the Word of God even if my convictions were wrong. Upon completion of my research, I am more convinced than ever that my convictions are in fact in line with the clear teachings of God's Word.

I believe that each of the chapters in this thesis add strength to my conclusion. Someone once compared the strength of an argument to a bundle of sticks. You may break one stick with some difficulty, but the strength of that stick increases exponentially by the number of sticks you add to the bundle. While I do not claim to have added all the sticks to this bundle, I do believe there is substantial evidence in all these chapters to cause any serious theologian to at least consider the results.

The key questions in chapter 1, which beg a solid answer, have been covered in the following chapters. I know of no other way to honestly answer these questions without a careful exegesis of God's Word. If we try to answer them out of personal bias or human reason, we are in danger of departing from biblical truth, which only leaves us with human opinion.

The story of the Old Quaker brings out the heart and purpose of this thesis which is, does God permit or cause death? There is a huge difference between these two concepts because if you make God the cause of death, He becomes the creator of evil and every hurtful thing which exists. The concept of cause says His sovereignty does not allow for real choice that would contain real options. The end result of the cause concept turns man into an automaton with no real purpose. It becomes God playing a game of chess with Himself and making us the pawns in the game which can only move when He moves us. The concept of permission, on the other hand, gives man the free will to choose between life and death.

Chapter 3 deals with the very biblical issue that says God the Father and God the Son are the same in purpose, mode of operation, and direction. To make the operation of God the Father different in the Old Testament by saying He kills or is in fact the cause of death goes against the entire purpose of the new covenant which is to redeem us from death!

The types and shadows dealt with in chapter 4 deals with some very important substantiation between the Old and the New Testaments. While the Old Testament is full of shadows of the New Testament, one must be very cautious not to add every detail of a type or shadow to prove a doctrine. To do so can lead to many misconceptions about who God is and what He is like. The old saying "the new is in the old concealed, and the old is in the new revealed" is still very true.

The principles of the kingdom of light and the kingdom of darkness dealt with in chapter 5 are, in my opinion, one of the most powerful evidences that these two kingdoms cannot be homogenized into a mixture of doctrine. Jesus Himself said they are two kingdoms which are entirely opposed, and they do not mix. To say that one is done by the power of the other is blasphemy against the Holy Spirit. That sounds like dangerous territory to me!

I believe that putting sickness and disease into God's will for us is an easy way to try to explain away the powerlessness of the church's condition in our generation. The other possibilities given in chapter 6 give us a more biblical reason for our ineffectiveness.

The Hebrew tenses which are explained in chapter 7 give room for the concept of permission, especially when God is speaking in the first person singular. I am convinced that because they can be translated as causation or permission and still be grammatically correct, the translation demonstrating permission is the only proper interpretation that is in line with the New Testament.

A proper syntactic is essential for a literal interpretation of the New Testament. The verses which I exegete in chapter 8 are essential for a clear understanding of the difficult Old Testament passages which appear to put causation on God for death and disease. I believe the scriptures I chose to bring out in chapter 8 from the New Testament add considerable evidence to the validity of this thesis.

The sovereignty of God and the free will of man must be brought into account as critical issues when dealing with permission verses causation. If one views sovereignty without considering God's legitimate granting of free will, then God indeed seems to be the primary source of evil. If one views man's free will apart from the scriptural view of sovereignty, then man becomes the only source of his destiny. Man's free will then must be the source of secondary causation.

Chapter 10 deals with a particular scriptural principle. It tells us that God's goodness produces faith. If one believes that God is the cause of evil, would that not logically produce unbelief? I added chapter 11 as a practical guide to help answer some legitimate questions people have about bad things that happen. Many times people blame God for evil because religion has taught things about God that are untrue.

Whatever your conclusion is on this subject, please understand that God is not your problem or the cause for your difficulty or hurt. God is a loving God who would never want you to bear the destruction caused by the fall of Adam's race. Jesus came to reverse the curse and start a new race. We are new creations in Christ and have left Adam's cursed race to be *in Christ* not *in Adam*.

> But now Christ is risen from the dead, and become the first fruits of those who have fallen asleep. For since by man came death, by Man also came the resurrection from the dead. For as IN ADAM all die, even so IN CHRIST all shall be made alive. (1 Corinthians 15:20–22)

ADDENDUM

Spiritual Principles Found in This Book

1. God and His commandment do not kill! Sin produces death and it does the killing. Romans 7:10–13. See page 110.
2. God's wrath is walking into His holiness without the protection of the blood of Christ. John 3:36. See page 111.
3. If you do not see that there is no darkness at all in God, then you do not know the difference between good and evil. I John 1:5, Genesis 3:5. See page 109.
4. Life choices bring life results from God. Death choices bring death results from the destroyer. Deuteronomy 28: 1, 2. 28:15, 30:14, 15, 19. See page 61.
5. God created the destroyer before he was the destroyer. Lucifer was created to worship God not to destroy or to carry out destruction. Destroyer or spoiler is what he became. Destruction is what is left when God's life is not chosen. Isaiah 14:12–15, 54:16, Ezekiel 28:12–13, I Corinthians 10:10. See page 99.
6. Preaching the goodness of God brings repentance; Conversely preaching the badness of God brings hardness of heart. Romans 2:4. See page 118.
7. Correct moral choice cannot be made without a correct absolute; Because it is the correct absolute which determines what is good and what is evil. Judges 21:25. See page 141.

8. Fairness itself says there must be an absolute in order to determine what is fair and what is not fair. Absolutes are in fact the process of order. Veracity is the process of reality. John 17:17. See page 142.

9. Real choices by definition must involve the chooser's options and they cannot be determined by the choice giver. To determine a choice negates the choice! Deuteronomy 30:19, 20. See page 108.

10. If Satan can get you to change your "God has said" to "has God said? He has moved you out of faith and into doubt. Genesis 3:1–4. See page 108.

11. God's wisdom is the ability to know the difference between good and evil. Isaiah 5:20–21, Genesis 3:5. See page 109.

12. What God is and what God does is not evil. God is a consuming fire. God's fire is His holiness. Hebrews 12:29. See page 109.

13. You become fireproof by the blood of Jesus Christ. Hebrews 10:9, 10. Page 83.

14. Christ does nothing under Satan's Kingdom. Matthew 12:25–28. See page 33.

15. What you honor come to you. What you dishonor goes from you. Exodus 20:12, Ephesians 6:2, Proverbs 3:9, 10, I Peter 3:7.

16. To be a life giver and a death giver would not be compatible with Biblical truth. John 10:10. See page 20.

17. In the natural realm light and darkness are opposites; The same is true in the spirit realm. Genesis 1:2–4. See page 34.

18. Right or wrong, "convinced" is the opposite of confusion; It is the substance of faith, it is the catalyst for action, it is the courage of all endeavors, If the substance is truth the result will be success, if the substance is error the result will be failure. The spirit of truth and error are the variables. I John 4:6. See page 37.

19. Expectation is the catalyst for miracles. Mark 9:23. See page 39.

20. Your concept of God will determine your theology. Lamentations 3:22–24. See page 118.
21. You can be right and still be wrong! I Corinthians 10:23, 24. See page 5.
22. Saving life is good, destroying life is evil. Luke 6:9. See page 100.
23. God's holiness is going to shake everything on this earth which is not under the blood of Christ; If you are a child of God His holiness will not shake you because His holiness is in you. Hebrews 12:25–29. See page 111.
24. God's goodness will give you back your hope. Jeremiah 29:11. See page 119.
25. God's goodness has eliminated your failure and given you Christ's righteousness. II Corinthians 5:21. See page 119.
26. God's goodness has destroyed the work of the accuser. Revelation 12:10. See page 119.
27. Every asset has a liability; man's free will is an asset given him by God but free will has the liability of consequences. Galatians 6:7. See page 126.
28. The believer who thoroughly understands that the power of God is backing him up can exercise his authority and face the enemy fearlessly. Mark 16:17–20. See page 129.
29. The reason we have not experienced the glory of God is because we have blamed God for that which is not good. Exodus 33:18–19. See page 146.
30. The goodness of God is synonymous with the glory of God. EXODUS 33:18, 19. See page 146.
31. Self-righteousness always leads people into the wilderness of failure. Exodus 19:8. See page 150.
32. In our dispensation of grace, God is giving people His righteousness instead of requiring their righteousness. Page 152.
33. Whenever darkness is turned into light it is exposed for what it is. Revelation 15:8–16. See page 153.
34. To the child of God His glory brings life; To the child of wrath our God who is a consuming fire become their kindling point of eternal destruction. See page 153.

35. God the Son would not do anything God the Father would not do; God the Father would not do anything God the Son would not do. John4:8–11. See page 20.

36. It is impossible to have faith for healing if you think God may or may not heal you. Faith must be based on the absolute that says you are healed. Isaiah 53:5, Mathew 8:17, I Peter 2:24. Page 103.

37. Two things Satan greatly fears are when God exalts one of His ministers and when one of his ministers is enlightened by revelation knowledge. II Corinthians 12:7. See page 101.

38. The God given right to choose is the very issue that made mankind redeemable. Free will is a God given right! See page 108.

39. Knowing good and evil is not the problem; Knowing the difference between the two is what has the world so messed up today. Isaiah 5:20, 21. See page 109.

40. The goodness of God makes you fall in love with your God. I John 4:19. See page 120.

41. Gift, grace, and favor are from the same Greek word which is "charis". See page 121.

42. Relationships stay strong when you feel valued by the person you are in relationship with. I John 4:19. See page 121.

43. Satan has nothing left to accuse you with. Revelation 12:10, Psalm 103:1–3. See page 121.

44. Every issue in life is a life or death choice! See page 146.

45. Culpability is on man's choice not on God's wonderful gift of free will. See page 127.

46. We who are Christians need to be the change that we desire to see in the world. See page 127.

47. The contemporary church needs no less authority today than it had in the first century. See page 128.

48. Your greatest failures are you ministry in reverse! See page 130.

49. To say God is tempting you with evil things is to break the commandment of God in James 1:13. See page 96.

50. The goodness of God cannot be changed. James 1:17. See page 99.

51. The Greek word for abundance is, "perisos", which means overflow. All true ministry is God's overflow in you. John 7:38. See page 98.

52. Death is an enemy and part of the fall. I Corinthians 15:26. See page 99.

53. Saving life is good. Destroying life is evil. Jesus always does good and never does evil. Luke 6:9. See page 100.

54. Christ's death destroyed the power of the devil. Hebrews 2:14. See page 101.

55. If God uses evil to teach us something, it would be treason against what Christ accomplished on the cross. Hebrews 2:14. See page 101.

56. The only affect Satan can have on a believer is to counterfeit, pervert, or usurp authority. Colossians 2:15. See page 101.

57. God never kills: Death is what kills. Revelation 2:23. See page 107.

58. Man's free will is the source of secondary causation. See page 114.

59. God's sovereignty and man's free will are completely compatible. See page 117.

60. Your prayers release the power of God over any situation. James 5:16. See page 117.

61. The word imputation is from the Greek word, "logizomai", It means to log onto an account. Romans 4:7–8. See page 119.

62. Mercy is when we do not get what we deserve. Grace is when we get what we do not deserve. Lamentations 3:22–23. See page 120.

63. Why did God let my child die is a question with a false assumption. The real question is why did my child die? See page 124.

64. God did not allow evil to come into the world. See page 126.

65. The letters for EVIL and LIVE are reverse in the English language. See page 127.

66. Always pray the Word; Always pray in the spirit; Always get results. See page 130.
67. There is a sin leading to death. I John 5:16–17. See page 133.
68. God thinks about you. Jeremiah 29:11. See page 137.
69. Dispensations in the Bible deal with God's stewardship in handling man sin and man's and man's responsibility for sin. See page 138.
70. Human government cannot bring world peace nor can it solve the world's problems. See page 145.
71. God's Word is a state of being. See page 146.
72. God needed to legally enter the human race of Adam in order to buy us back. See page 146.
73. God's law makes nothing perfect. Hebrews 7:19. See page 149.
74. Both the goodness of God and the glory of God are inseparable. See page 146.
75. The Old Testament and the New Testament are in complete agreement with each other. See page 24.
76. I submit that it is not only dangerous but also hermeneutically improper to try to give God an attribute that does not line up with New Testament teaching. See page 28.
77. "To transgress His boundaries is to receive what is to receive what is on the other side of His property line, death." See page 29.
78. "Convinced", is the opposite of confusion. See page 37.

BIBLIOGRAPHY

Arndt, William F. and F. Wilbur Gingrich. *A Greek-English Lexicon of the New Testament and Other Early Christian Literature.* The University of Chicago Press: Cambridge at the University Press, 1952.

Bevere, John. *The Bait of Satan: Living Free from the Deadly Trap of Offense.* Charisma House, 2014.

Carson, D. A. *How Long, O Lord? Reflections on Suffering and Evil.* 2nd ed. Grand Rapids, MI: Baker Book House, 2006. Print.

Cloud, Dr. Henry and Dr. John Townsend. *Boundaries.* Grand Rapids, Michigan: Zondervan Publishing House, 1992.

Dana, H. E. and Julius R. Mantey, TH.D., D.D. *A Manual Grammar of the Greek New Testament.* Toronto, Ontario, Canada: The Macmillan Company, 1927.

David Ingles. "I Am the Righteousness of God (In Christ)." *There's a Whole Lot of People Going Home.* David Ingles Music. Tulsa, Oklahoma, 1976.

Douglas, J. D. *The New International Dictionary of the Christian Church.* Revised ed. Grand Rapids Michigan: Zondervan Publishing House, 1974, 1978.

Good, Joseph. *Rosh HaShanah and the Messianic Kingdom to Come: An Interpretation of the Feast of Trumpets.* Hatikva Ministries, 1989.

Hagin, Kenneth E. *The Believer's Authority.* 2nd ed. Tulsa, OK: Thirty-Third Printing, 2005. Print.

———. *Seven Things You Should Know About Divine Healing.* Tulsa, Oklahoma: Kenneth Hagin Ministries, 1983.

Heick, Otto W. *A History of Christian Thought.* Philadelphia, Pennsylvania: Fortress Press, 1965.

Holy Bible, New King James Version. (Unless otherwise noted).

Kaiser, Walter C. Jr. *Hard Sayings of the Bible*. Downers Grove, IL: InterVarsity, 1996.

————. *Toward Old Testament Ethics*. Grand Rapids, Michigan: Academic Books, Zondervan Publishing House, 1983.

Metzger, Bruce M. and Allen Wickgren. *The Greek New Testament*. London, England: United Bible Societies, 1966.

Nelson, Thomas Inc. *The New King James Bible*. Korea: Thomas Nelson Inc., 1982.

Simonds, Robert, et al. *The Pink Panther*. Sony Pictures Releasing, 2006.

Towns, Elmer L. *Theology for Today*. Belmont, California: Thomson Learning Inc., 2002.

Virkler, Henry A. *Hermeneutics, Principles, and Processes of Biblical Interpretation*. Grand Rapids, Michigan: Baker Book House Company, 1981.

West, Matthew. "Do Something."_Nashville, Tennessee: Sparrow Records, 2012.

Yates, Kyle M., PhD. *The Essentials of Biblical Hebrew*. Louisville, Kentucky: Harper and Row Publishers.

Zodhiates, Dr. Spiros. *The Complete Word Study Old Testament, King James Version*. Chattanooga, Tennessee: AMG Publishers, 1994.

Zondervan Publishing House. *The Amplified New Testament*. Grand Rapids Michigan: Zondervan Publishing House, 1958.

————. *The Analytical Greek Lexicon*. Grand Rapids, Michigan: Zondervan Publishing House, 1970.

ABOUT THE AUTHOR

Pastor Maffucci is a 1970 graduate of Moody Bible Institute where he studied pastoral theology and majored in New Testament Greek. After graduating from Moody, he did further studies at Tennessee Temple University and Hyles Anderson College.

After being baptized in the Holy Spirit in 1973, he studied under the ministry of Dr. Bob Yandian in Tulsa, Oklahoma, and was ordained under Grace Fellowship in Tulsa. He has been a pastor for over fifty years and has started three churches.

He is presently ordained under Pastor J. B. Whitfield at Agape Faith Church in Clemmons, North Carolina.

Pastor Maffucci holds a bachelor of theology and a master of theology degree from Impact University where he has been an instructor in New Testament Greek and Bible Theology since 2009. He is now completing a doctorate in theology from Life Christian University.